Superpower
5.0

Dedication

◆◆◆

To You…

Through every struggle,
Rest in this absolute truth,
You are a hero.

It takes a village…

I would like to thank the many people who helped bring Superpower 5.0 to the world. I'll start with Robyn, my editor, with her deep and critical eye. Then there's John, the creative genius behind the cover. Both of you are impossibly patient and consummate professionals.

Thank you, Andrea, Batch, Charles, Dale, Janet, Ken, Karen, Kathy, Marc, Mark, Sarah, Wendy, and Will, for your personal contributions to this book. Some of you served as beta-readers of the ealry manuscript and some of you were kind enough to allow me to share parts of your personal superpower journey within these pages. It's been an honor and a blast working with each of you!

My list wouldn't be complete without thanking my beautiful wife Kathie. Not only does she put up with me, which is a superpower in itself; she is always there, standing right behind me, with kind words of encouragement, as I do my work in the world. I love you.

Superpower 5.0

The 5-Point Plan
for Designing the
Best Version of Yourself

Mike Herzog

Someritus LLC

PO Box 54, Lafayette, Indiana, 47902

Published in the United States

By Someritus LLC
ISBN: 978-1-7340620-2-1: (Kindle)
ISBN: 978-1-7340620-3-8: (Paperback)

Developmental Editing by Robyn Passante
Cover Design by John Bulmer
(www.bulmerphotography.com)

Contents

◆◆◆

Getting to 5.0

BOOK THREE - THE REWARD

PROLOGUE - THE FINAL FRONTIER

The Full Experience

◆◆◆

I'm going to start with a confession. I'm a terrible, irresponsible reader. Downright reprehensible. I always skip the Preface. I know; it's unforgivable. I'm probably missing half the point of the book. It's just that my attention span is so damn short these days. I want to get right to the point.

Here is the point:

This book comes with a **Digital Appendix**.

I do ask that you provide your email address to access the Digital Appendix. I won't lie to you. This request is selfishly motivated. I'm excited about the opportunity to share my work with you. I hope you'll find that it serves you well and I hope you'll stick around. That said, I want to make a sacred promise to you…

- I will never share your email address with anyone.
- I will not bombard you with emails.
- I will never make high-pressure sales pitches.
- I will always make it super-easy for you to opt-out of my mailing list and I won't take it personally if you choose to step away. And I'll always welcome you back with open arms.

I don't consider the Digital Appendix to be a bonus. In my mind, it's crucial. Superpower 5.0 is more than just a book. It's more than just an exercise of the brain. Superpower 5.0 is designed to be a fully engaging experience, and the Digital Appendix is a huge part of that. In it you'll find dozens of ways to deepen your understanding and enhance your learning. You'll find helpful self-assessment tools, downloadable worksheets, access to superpower discovery interviews, and much more.

I recommend you claim your Digital Appendix right now, at: www.superpower50.com

Real-Life Examples

 People always want me to share examples of real-life superpowers, so I've included a number of examples in this book and even more in the Digital Appendix. That said, I have some apprehensions about providing too many examples, and here's why.

The superpower journey is an incredibly personal one and I consider it a privilege to have worked with so many individuals to design their superpower. The decision to share one's personal superpower work with the world is a generous decision, and I am eternally grateful to the people who've agreed to let me share their stories. I do not take this lightly.

Because the superpower process is such a personal one, there's always something lost in translation whenever you share your superpower with someone else, or when someone else shares theirs with you. The only way to truly experience the power of the process is to come up with your own superpower. So, there's risk in sharing examples with you before you've had your own experience.

I've chosen to limit the number of examples that I provide in the book because I worry that it will create undue influence on your own design process. I tried to include just enough examples to illustrate the key points, but no more. By putting additional examples in the Digital Appendix, it allows you to go through your own discovery process and then circle back to the examples to draw additional inspiration, which you can use to upgrade your work.

***

Additional Resources
You can access your Digital Appendix here:
www.superpower50.com

BOOK ONE

—

THE CHALLENGE

Where Am I Now?

◆◆◆

Congratulations! If you've picked up this book, it probably means you've already overcome the first challenge. It means you are open to the idea that superpowers exist and that you might actually have one. Trust me, overcoming this first challenge is a big deal.

So many people are living in a state of denial. They either don't believe that "ordinary" people have superpowers, or they simply don't think it's possible they have one. Unfortunately, this means they will never fully discover or embrace their authenticity. It means they will never realize their full potential. It means they will never experience the full vibrancy that life has to offer.

But you picked up this book. You've already started your superpower journey. It's a journey that many people, just like you, have undertaken. Although each journey is different, they are fundamentally similar. In my experience, working with hundreds of people to help them unlock and unleash their superpower, there are a few common stages that people experience. I've used these stages to provide the structure of this book.

Have a look at these descriptions and see if you can determine where you might be in your journey:

Superpower Version 0.0 - You are in total denial about the idea of superpowers, as least the idea that you might have one.

Superpower Version 1.0 - You have an idea what your superpower might be, but you're not entirely sure. The words you use to describe your superpower are okay, but they don't light a fire in your belly. You may be uncomfortable sharing your superpower with others.

Superpower Version 2.0 - You've found language to describe your superpower that really pops. When you think about your superpower, you feel a sense of excitement and motivation. You are starting to get more comfortable telling people about your superpower, and you are eager to find ways to start using it.

Superpower Version 3.0 - Your superpower is a vital part of your life. Your superpower is doing real work on your behalf, every day. You are very conscious of when you are using your superpower and when you are not. You actively use your superpower to make decisions, both short-term and long-term.

Superpower Version 4.0 - You are actively working to optimize your superpower. You have regular practices for stretching yourself and improving your superpower execution. You are acutely aware of the limits and limitations of your superpower and you work to mitigate those. You know when your superpower gets you into trouble and you work to avoid those situations. Your superpower is very strong, but you know it can always be stronger.

Superpower Version 5.0 - Your life purpose and your superpower are indistinguishable. You use your superpower to improve the lives of others and you actively encourage other people to discover their superpower.

If you're not quite sure where you are on your superpower journey, I've included a short survey that will help you figure it out. You can access this survey in the Digital Appendix.

The Road Ahead

Later on, in *Book Two - The Adventure*, we'll go deeply into each of the five superpower stages. Each stage has it's own subsection: *Getting to 1.0, Getting to 2.0, Getting to 3.0*, etc.

I recommend you read each subsection, even if you already think you know which stage you are in right now. Although you may have already passed through some stages, it's likely that you'll find interesting details and nuances that may not have occurred to you. You might even enjoy doing some of the practices and exercises in the Digital Appendix as a refresher.

That's it for the dos and don'ts. It's time to buckle up. It's going to be one heck of a ride.

***

Additional Resources

Check out the **Where Am I Now?**
self-assessment survey in the Digital Appendix.

www.superpower50.com

A Story of Hope

◆◆◆

The only person you are destined to become
is the person you decide to be.
- Ralph Waldo Emerson

When I first began exploring the concept of superpower, I was driven by a single, hopeful premise:

Every single person has a superpower.
They may not know it. They may not understand it.
But everyone has one.
And the world will be a better place when each one of us
discovers the true nature of our superpower
and then starts using it in the world.

To test this premise, I started my investigation close to home. If I couldn't name my own superpower, then how could I possibly expect other people to name theirs? Fortunately, I had a head start because I've spent a significant portion of my time and attention over the past decade doing deep, self-reflective work. Although I had never used the word "superpower" to describe myself, as soon as I did, it felt completely natural. Like a favorite pair of jeans. A perfect fit. Here it is, my superpower: *I am a bridge between body and soul.*

There. I said it. After five different revisions of this book, that's the first time I've written those words. Until this point, I was hesitant to write them. Who am I to declare myself to have such a lofty superpower? What evidence do I have that I am a bridge between body and soul? Come to think of it, what the heck does that even mean?

And herein lies the first lesson about discovering your superpower. It doesn't matter what other people think. Your superpower is about you and what you think. It's about what you know about yourself. The ultimate value of your superpower isn't that others find it impressive. The ultimate value of your superpower is that you find it useful. The value is in the fuel that your superpower provides, for your body, and for your soul.

Your superpower is clarity. It is direction. It is inspiration. It is you. Only you.

Somewhere inside of you there is a superpower.

It's my job to help you find it.

A Story of Resistance

◆◆◆

Most of us have two lives. The life we live, and the unlived life within us. Between the two stands Resistance.
- Steven Pressfield, Author of *The War of Art*

If everyone has a superpower, then why aren't more people talking about it? Why doesn't everyone walk around with a badge on their chest, proudly declaring their superpower to the world? Why did it take me four decades to name my own superpower? Why did it take me five drafts of this book to summon the courage to tell you about it?

Fear.

It's that simple. Steven Pressfield calls it "Resistance," but he's really talking about fear. Most of us are afraid to seriously consider the idea that we have a superpower so we avoid talking about it. Instead, we tell ourselves the same sad stories designed to keep us living in the perceived safety of our default lives.

See if this feels familiar...

Only superheroes have superpowers and I'm no hero. I'm not special. Look at me. I've never been the world's best ... anything, despite what that coffee mug on my desk says. I am utterly ordinary.

I'm just a mother.
I'm just a barista.
I'm just a lawyer.
I'm just a janitor.

I'm just a waiter.
I'm just a restaurant owner.
I'm just a retired accountant.
I'm just a dentist.
I'm just a struggling artist.
I'm just a farmer.
I'm just the assistant to the regional manager.

Each of us has told our own version of the same story.

Here's the thing. I've met amazing people who are living each of those lives. In each and every case, I could appreciate the commitment and pride they brought to their work. Although I was not always privy to their struggles, I know that every one of them had struggles. We all do. It's part of living. Everyone struggles in their own, unique way.

Each of these people is a hero.

So am I.

So are you.

You are not "just" anything.

An Unlikely Role Model

◆◆◆

Children see magic because they look for it.
- Christopher Moore, American author

Over the years, I've found that one demographic doesn't experience Resistance around the idea of a personal superpower—kids under the age of ten. Ask a seven-year-old if they have a superpower and they'll ask you how much time you have. It's amazing. It's inspiring.

Here's the sad thing. Ask a teenager if they have a superpower. They might give you an answer, but the chances drop precipitously. When I ask older kids, something strange happens. Instead of an immediate and enthusiastic response, I'm more likely to get a blank stare. I'm more likely to hear "I don't know" or "I don't have one." It's heartbreaking.

What happens to us around age 10? Do superpowers diminish with age?

Of course not. It has nothing to do with our aging bodies. The problem is in our minds.

Your mind changes. Your priorities change. Your superpower fades when you start to care what other people think. More precisely, you push your superpower into the background. Don't feel bad, we all do it.

When we're young, our sense of identity comes from the same place as our sense of wonder, the same place as our imagination—inside of us. As we get older, we derive our sense of identity from the people around us.

We look to our friends, our family, our teachers. *Tell me who I am. Tell me who I'm not.*

Why can't we see ourselves? Why can't we be ourselves?

We surrender the one thing that is truly ours—our authenticity.

The Desire to Belong

◆◆◆

Why fit in when you were born to stand out?
- Dr. Seuss

Comic book superheroes often live two separate lives. There's millionaire Bruce Wayne, a.k.a. Batman. Peter Parker lived a perfectly normal life until he got bitten by a radioactive spider, which allowed him to become Spiderman. And who could forget the lovable Clark Kent? Beneath that boring tie was a blazing letter "S".

Take a look at these three pairings. One of them is not like the other two.

Bruce Wayne : Batman
Peter Parker : Spiderman
Clark Kent : Superman

Can you spot the outlier?

Within the world of fictional superheroes, which of the three were the "real" people and which were the alter-egos?

Bruce Wayne was the real person and Batman was the alter-ego. Peter Parker was the real person and Spiderman was his alter-ego. But what about Superman? Was he Clark Kent's alter-ego? Nope. Recall Superman's origin story...

Kal-El, as he was named at birth, came to Earth as a baby. Jonathan and Martha Kent found him, adopted him, and gave him the name Clark. They sent him to school like a normal kid. He was a superhero hiding in plain sight.

Think about it. Superman didn't need to wear glasses. Clark Kent wore glasses so people wouldn't recognize him for who he really was.

Why the charade?

The Kents wanted Clark to be like every other kid. They wanted him to fit in. So did Clark. Even when he reached adulthood, Clark went to great strides to hide his true identity. On some level, he didn't want to be different.

Most of us are living our own version of a Clark Kent alter-ego. We convince ourselves that we are not special. We convince ourselves that it's better to fit in than to stand out. We convince ourselves it's not worth the trouble. If we discover that we have a superpower, it will come with all kinds of obligations attached. *Who needs that kind of responsibility?*

Instead, we allow our superpower to remain hidden. We deny its existence, even to ourselves. We go about our life as Clark Kent and we convince ourselves that it's real. We convince ourselves that it's okay.

It's not okay.

We convince ourselves that we're ordinary.

I am not ordinary.

Neither are you.

Ordinary is a Choice

◆◆◆

Never love anyone who treats you like you're ordinary.
- Oscar Wilde

Clark Kent wants to convince us that ordinary is desirable. He wants to convince us that ordinary is inevitable. There's nothing else out there for us so we should just stop thinking about it. I love ya Clark, but you're wrong.

Ordinary is a choice.

It's the choice to stop trying.

Ordinary is remaining quiet when you know you should speak up.

Ordinary is walking past a piece of trash on the street and pretending you don't see it. It's leaving the problem for someone else to pick up. It's hoping that someone else will care enough to *do* something about it.

Ordinary is doing the bare minimum.

Ordinary is "good enough."

Ordinary is playing safe.

Ordinary is sitting when everyone else is dancing.

Ordinary is sitting back when you know, deep down, you should engage.

Ordinary is doing less than you can, and knowing it.

Ordinary is being less than you can be, and knowing it.

Ordinary is a choice.

Your superpower is a choice too.

Your superpower is the antidote to ordinary.

A Fond Farewell

◆ ◆ ◆

It's time to say goodbye to Clark Kent.

You've served us well, my friend, but your services are no longer needed. We've got it from here.

It's time to name and claim your superpower.

The moment you do, everything changes. Life will never be the same. I'm not saying life will be easy. It won't. But it will be more vibrant. It will be more meaningful. It will be true.

Right now, right here, you are standing in front of a stone. Buried in that stone is a sword. Grab hold. Draw it from that granite grip. Liberate it. Liberate your greatness.

This is where the adventure begins.

BOOK TWO

—

THE ADVENTURE

What is a Superpower?

◆◆◆

The reason most people struggle to identify their superpower is they begin with a flawed mental model. They define "superpower" in a way that makes it virtually impossible to achieve. What is your definition of superpower? Maybe it looks a bit like this:

Something that I can do that nobody else can do.

Do you see the inherent flaw? It's utterly unachievable. In a world of 7 billion people, unless you can fly, see through walls, or happen to have a lasso of truth, there's going to be someone else who can do what you do. This definition doesn't work.

What if we define superpower as being "the best" at something? How would that be? Better? Not really. First off, what does "the best" even mean?

What does it mean to be the best teacher? The best writer? The best parent? The best barista? The best anything? It's subjective. "Best" relies on someone else's measurement and someone else's judgment. Is Michael Jordan the best basketball player of all time? LeBron James fans might have something to say about that. If the Eagles have the best-selling album of all time, does that make it the best? Not in my playlist.

Even if we can identify "the best" as an objective measure, there will always be someone out there who's better than we are. They may even be sitting at the desk right next to ours. If we hold out trying to find something that we're the best at doing, we'll spend our entire lives disappointed. We'll be in a constant state of failing to live up and of knowing that we're not the best.

Having a superpower doesn't mean we're the best.

We need a better definition of superpower and it needs to do three things. (1) It needs to differentiate us, (2) in a meaningful way and (3) it needs to be universally accessible. I would like to offer a new definition:

Superpower:
The way you do
what you do
that's uniquely you.

Take a few moments to notice what this definition does not include. It doesn't mention achieving specific results. That would simply put us right back into the morass of subjectivity. This definition of superpower doesn't focus on *what* you do, rather it highlights the *way* you do it.

Uniqueness lies at the heart of your superpower. Although there will be many people who do *what* you do, there will only be one person who does it the *way* that you do it. In this sense, your superpower is akin to a fingerprint, or a signature. Similar to everyone else's, yet truly unique.

No two people have the exact same superpower because no two people are exactly the same. In order to discover your superpower, you must first embrace a core principle:

You are unique and that uniqueness matters.

Most people have an easier time with the first part of that statement. We know that no other person has the same genetics, the same life experiences, the same values, or the same motivations. It's easy to believe that each of us is unique.

The second part is a bit more challenging. It's more difficult to appreciate our uniqueness. To see it as a useful differentiator. To see it as a superpower. Making that mental shift is ultimately what this book is all about. We need to appreciate that we do things differently than everyone else around us, even though it may appear to the outside observer that we are doing the exact same thing. We need to see the beauty in what makes our *way* different.

The first step is to realize, in your mind, and in your heart, that your *way* is unique.

To do that, we have to identify your *way*.

A Different Approach

◆◆◆

In the last chapter I shared a new definition of superpower. One that requires a mental shift for most people. Now I'd like to offer another mental shift that you'll need to make if you are to continue on this superpower journey. To begin, I'd like to pose a question.

Where does a person's superpower come from? I'm not asking about *your* superpower. In general, where do superpowers come from? Take a few minutes to consider this, then come back. I'll wait right here.

Did you conclude that superpowers are something innate for each person? Call it genetics. Call it a gift from God. Most people sense that superpower is something that comes from within.

I agree. A huge part of one's superpower comes from within. I also think that our environment is a contributing factor. It's the classic, "nature vs. nurture" argument. The answer is always the same: yes, and…

It's the unique combination of nature and nurture that allows every person, all 7-billion plus of us, to have a unique superpower.

So, we all have a unique superpower inside of us, and we just need to discover it, right?

Not exactly.

Superpower isn't just about discovery, it's largely about design.

What does it mean to design something? In my first book, *Never Too Late*, I describe "design" as having two primary elements: **Intention** and **Iteration**. In other words, design requires a high degree of purpose and focus (intention). Design also requires trial and error (iteration).

To realize your superpower, you should think about it as a design project. There will be an element of discovery, no doubt. But that discovery will happen as a result of your intention and your iteration.

Why is this important? Why does it matter whether we think about the superpower process as discovery or as design?

Discovery is a function of outcome. Thus, discovery is subject to chance. You may find something, you may not. It depends on where you look and what you are looking for. When it comes to discovery, there are no guarantees.

Design, on the other hand, is guaranteed.

You have a superpower. I know that and I suspect, on some level, you do too. Design isn't some magical process whereby you go from zero to hero in an instant. Design is a constant building and shaping that gets better and better every single day.

When does it end?

It never ends.

Getting to 1.0

◆◆◆

For some people, the first step of superpower design is the hardest. Going from version zero to version 1.0. Going from absolutely nothing to potentially something. Going from *I have no idea,* to *I think there's a chance my superpower is…*

The gap between zero and 1.0 is huge. But why?

I think there are two reasons. The first reason is the easy explanation. It's the one that most people will give if you ask them why they can't name their superpower: *I simply have no idea what my superpower is.* And this may be true. It's a brilliant argument because it's impossible to refute. I don't know what you don't know. But I suspect that you probably know more than you're letting on. You probably know more than you think you know.

The second reason why it's so hard to go from zero to 1.0 is a bit subtler. The reason lies in your subconscious mind. It's possible that you subconsciously feel pressure to "get it right." You don't want to name something as your superpower only to discover you got it wrong. Rather than get it wrong, you'd rather wait until you have it right.

I'm going to let you in on a little secret. You won't get it right. Not the first time, anyway. Heck, you may never get it exactly right. It doesn't matter. It especially doesn't matter in the beginning, when it's not about right versus wrong, it's about nothing versus something. Don't worry about getting it right. You've got a lifetime to get it right.

Are you feeling clueless about what your superpower might be? Are you sensing the pressure to get it right the first time? If so, then you'll want to spend some time in the *Getting to 1.0* section. Getting to 1.0 is about answering this simple question:

What is my superpower?

Again, we're not trying to answer this question with absolute certainty. When it comes to superpower design, there's no such thing, because each of us is a work-in-progress. But we do need to come up with some kind of answer, at least to get the ball rolling. To do this, we'll be exploring different techniques for looking at your life in a new light so that you can begin to identify your superpower.

If you already have a sense of what your superpower may be, then you can probably come up with a response to the question above. You might find the *Getting to 1.0* section is slowing you down. Feel free to skim through these chapters quickly. You can always dive deep if you come across something that piques your interest. Chances are, even if you've been thinking about your superpower for a while, one or two of the techniques in this section will be novel to you and give you a fresh perspective.

Start Where You Are

◆◆◆

If you have absolutely no idea what your superpower may be, where is the best place to start looking for it? My answer to this is simple … start where you are.

You might resist the idea that your current life is the best place to look for your superpower. To some extent, it's your current life that you are seeking to change by designing your superpower. How would it feel to discover that your superpower has been right here, under your nose, for all these years? It's hard to imagine, but it's true. The best place to start is where you are right now.

There's an old adage "It's difficult to see the picture when you are inside the frame." In order to see the picture, you need to first step out of the frame. Once you do, you'll see yourself in a completely new way.

Even if you see your life as dull, you will discover flashes of brilliance. Don't kid yourself, you've had them. You've overcome obstacles. You've endured hardships. You've had your finest moments. Chances are, some version of your superpower was at work during those times.

You didn't get here entirely by chance. We attract the life that we have.

We gravitate toward environments, roles, and relationships based on our strengths and preferences. Even if you think you've ended up in a place entirely by chance, if you look closely (and honestly), you will notice the ways that you attracted your reality. Don't roll your eyes. This isn't something magical or mystical. I'm not talking about simply "manifesting" a Ferrari into your garage. I'm saying that we have a lot more influence than we sometimes care to admit. I'm also not completely dismissing the impact of random events; but these don't define our life. It's our reaction to life events that ultimately shapes our reality, not the events themselves.

No matter what is happening in your life right now, your superpower is present. Its effects may be subtle to the point of near invisibility, but they are there. We leave our fingerprints on everything we touch with our life. We sign our name to everything that we do.

If you pay attention, if you look very closely, chances are you'll see traces of your superpower.

"The Way" Points the Way

◆◆◆

Remember the new definition of superpower:

The way you do — what you do — that is uniquely you.

Don't get hung up on *what* you are doing right now. Most of us have been doing what we're doing for a long time. That means it feels familiar. It feels ordinary. Most of us associate our identity with the "what" of our lives. I'm a bank teller. I'm a bus driver. I'm an ER nurse.

What we are doing doesn't usually reveal our unique superpower, because the "what" is circumstantial. To discover your superpower, don't focus on the "what." Focus on the *way*.

An Important Disclaimer

At this point, I need to call something to your attention. To illustrate a concept, I'm going to focus on the realm of "work." In my experience, work is a realm of life that resonates with most people and also consumes a significant portion of our energy, day to day. This is not to say that superpower is purely a professional endeavor. Your superpower may have nothing to do with whatever you do for a living. For the purposes of superpower discussion, I just find it easiest to use examples from the vocational realm.

With that out of the way, let's proceed.

Identifying Your Way

Each of us has a unique way of doing what we do. Our signature style. This is true, even if there are twenty other people in the office who have the exact same job title. It's true, even if there are thousands, or millions, of people in the world who would say they do the exact same thing. Nobody does it exactly the same way that you do it.

To discover this, you need to look very closely. You'll have to look beneath the surface by asking yourself questions that force you to explore the depths. Asking yourself questions helps you to step out of the frame so you can see the picture of your life.

This is where having other people around you with similar roles can help. What makes your way of doing the thing different from theirs? Don't get hung up on who does it better, because that can be arbitrary and also circumstantial. Simply notice what makes you different. Your initial reaction may be to say "nothing." But is that really true? Is that how you really feel? I don't think I've ever met anyone who would honestly say they are *exactly* like everyone else around them. That's just Resistance talking. Let's tease this out a bit further.

Are there specific details that matter to you that don't seem to matter to everyone else? You may find yourself saying "I wouldn't do it that way." When you notice that your approach is different from everyone else's, it's worth looking deeper into the reason why. You might have an epiphany about how your *way* is unique.

Once you start to develop a sense of your uniqueness, it's helpful to test your differential diagnosis by bouncing your observations off other people. You'll need to get curious about the people around you to see what makes them tick. Understanding the people around us can help us to better understand ourselves.

Do you often receive compliments about something in particular? It's possible that people are picking up on something that you do differently than what they typically encounter. Noticing how other people experience us can provide insight into what makes our signature unique. Pull on those threads a bit and see if they're connected to something bigger.

When you discuss your work with your colleagues, do you notice differences in the things they care about and the things that matter to you? Do you often disagree with the people around you? What is the source of those differences and disagreements?

One of the best ways to discover your superpower is to use fresh eyes to examine your life as it stands today. Chances are, your superpower is making an appearance in the *way* you do things and it's happening right under your nose.

The next two chapters will give you some specific techniques for seeing your life with fresh eyes.

What Makes You Proud?

◆◆◆

Your superpower is something that makes you different from everyone around you. In the early stages of superpower design, this creates a subtle problem. I'm guessing you have a healthy sense of humility, which means you probably have a slight allergy when it comes to differentiating yourself from everyone else. If you're different, that might imply you are better, which feels arrogant. No good. We need to approach this from a slightly different angle.

What are you most proud of?

We take pride in the things that make us different from the rest. We're proud of the high-quality work that we create because we know what it means to do work of lesser quality. We're proud of our child who got straight A's on their report card because we know that's not easy and it's not the norm. We're proud of our country, whichever country that may be, because we recognize that not every country has what we have. Without differentiation, there is no pride.

This means that pride gets a bad rap, sometimes. Pride, taken too far, is akin to narcissism. But healthy pride is nothing more than a deep pleasure and satisfaction in who we are, what we've done, and what we're doing. There's nothing wrong with a healthy sense of pride. I'm proud of myself for saying that.

Consider your life. Consider your work. Consider your contributions beyond work. Consider your family and your friends. I'm certain there are things in your life that spark pride. Follow those sparks.

Pride always points us to something that we value. It's easy to get hung up on the tangible things that serve as the visible target for our pride. Your house. Your spouse. That straight-A report card your kid brought home last week. That plastic bowling trophy you won a couple years ago. But if you look closely, you'll probably find that it's not the *things* that give you pride. Pride isn't about the outputs, it's about the inputs. The effort. The commitment. The love. The things you put in, not the things you get out.

This is where you may find connections between pride and your superpower. As you identify your proudest moments, ask yourself a few questions: What are the values that I hold dear? What was my contribution to this proud moment? What did I put into the system that was uniquely me? It's quite possible that your superpower was at work in those moments.

The areas of our life that give us the most pride tell us what matters most. What matters most often differentiates us from everyone else. Oftentimes our superpower is what makes the difference.

So, what makes you proud?

What Makes You Move?

If a man does not keep pace with his companions,
perhaps it is because he hears the beat of a different drummer.
- Henry David Thoreau

Do you often find yourself dancing to the beat of a different drummer? If so, have you ever wondered why? It might be your superpower that makes you move to a different beat than everyone else. What makes you move?

Another way to ask this question is to ask … How do you measure success?

At the end of the day, how do you know if you had a good day or a bad one? How do you know if you're on the right track? My guess is you've never bothered to look at *how* you know whether you had a good day or a bad day. You just *know* whether it was good, bad, or somewhere in between. Unfortunately, this means that you don't know how to replicate the good days and avoid the bad. It's really useful to notice how you measure the difference.

Okay, but what does this have to do with my superpower?

Quite possibly, nothing. I'm sorry to put it bluntly. None of these techniques are guaranteed to point directly to your superpower. Designing one's superpower is incredibly personal. I'll be sharing some techniques, or tools, but not every one of these tools will be the right tool for you. My recommendation is to play around with all of them and see which work the best for you. Now, back to work.

We were talking about how you measure success in your life. You may not realize this, but not everyone measures success the same way. Of course, you understand this logically, but how often do you pay attention to the differences between the way you measure success and the ways everyone else measures success?

At this point, I want to share an example because it illustrates how someone can find themselves marching to the beat of a different drummer.

A Different Drummer - Meet Ken

Ken is a senior project manager in a large consulting firm. He's smart, talented, and hard-working, all of which have contributed to his success over the years. Ken's career progression followed a predictable path. With each successful project, Ken's bosses would ensure his next assignment was even more complex and more challenging. As his bosses raised the bar, Ken continued to step up to the challenge.

Slowly, Ken began noticing that he was losing passion for the job. As his motivation dropped, so did his attention to detail. From time to time, the quality of his work slipped, ever so slightly. Ken noticed this and recognized it was not consistent with his usual way of operating, so he became curious to figure out what was going on.

As Ken began looking closely at his work, he began to notice differences in the way that he measured success for himself and the way that his company measured success for someone in his role.

Ken discovered that his favorite days were the ones where he got to work closely with the junior members of the project team, helping them to overcome their technical challenges. Ken realized that he preferred being an advisor and mentor to other people more than he cared about solving his own technical problems. As Ken began to explore his superpower, he realized that it was around developing people, not solving technical problems.

Ken identified his superpower as: *Inviting people to flourish.*

As it happens, Ken's employer looks at the world a bit differently. For someone with Ken's job title, the organization tends to place more emphasis on solving technical problems than on mentoring and advising junior people. Although there's nothing inherently wrong with this approach, it was creating some tension in Ken's life that he needed to address.

Once Ken began looking at his work through the lens of his superpower, things became much clearer. Ken also came up with some useful language to describe the tension he was feeling, and he was able to use this language to discuss the problem with his bosses.

Upon hearing about Ken's superpower, did his bosses immediately revamp their performance model to meet Ken's needs? Did they instantly reshape Ken's role so that he could focus exclusively on mentoring and growing less-experienced employees? Of course not. But they were receptive to the idea and now Ken and his bosses are working together to find roles that will benefit everyone involved.

Was it easy? No. Did it happen overnight? No way. But now Ken is moving in the right direction and it may not have happened if he hadn't noticed that his measures of personal success had shifted and were different from the people around him.

Listen to Your Drummer

How do the people around you, the people who are doing the same thing as you, measure success? How about the people for whom you work? How about the people you are trying to serve? How are your ways of measuring success different from theirs? How might these differences point to your superpower?

Your superpower is closely associated with your talents, but it's also deeply connected to your values. Noticing how you march differently from the people around you is a great way to identify what you value.

If you find yourself marching to the beat of a different drummer, you need to talk to that drummer.

***

Additional Resources

Check out the **Start Where You Are** exercise in the Digital Appendix.

www.superpower50.com

Look Everywhere

◆◆◆

How you do anything is how you do everything.
- Unknown

This quote, which is often attributed to Zen Buddhism, has some interesting implications for superpower design.

Over the past 10 years of coaching senior executives, I can't count the number of times I've had a client tell me "that's how I operate at work, but in the other areas of my life, I'm a different person." Rarely does a person have such distinction in their life. We are complete humans, not robots with specialized components for specific jobs. We are who we are, everywhere we go. This has important implications for your superpower design.

Your superpower is rarely confined to a single area of your life. Your superpower is fundamental to you. It's at your very core. Your superpower can show up anywhere, so every aspect of your life is worth examining.

If your work doesn't feel interesting or relevant to you, start your search somewhere else. Someplace where you feel more energy. Anything to get the ideas flowing. Momentum is your friend.

When it comes to superpower design, no aspect of your life is off-limits. If work isn't working, start with your personal life. Relationships. Passion projects. Hobbies. All of these can provide insights into who you are and what you value.

There's a good chance you'll be able to identify your superpower by noticing the *way* that you engage in the most important areas of your life.

Okay, great. But how do I do that, exactly?

The next few chapters will explain where and how to look for your *way*.

Look to the Past

◆◆◆

Most of us spend too much time on the last twenty-four hours and too little on the last six thousand years.
- Will Durant

I like this quote because it reminds us about the value of our past. It may feel counterintuitive that your past has anything to offer in terms of helping you discover your superpower. After all, if the answer was in the past, wouldn't you already know the answer? Not necessarily.

In the past, there was a problem—You didn't know what you were looking for.

Luckily, we have the opportunity to do look again, with the benefit of hindsight. You need to tap into the rich database of life experiences and look for signs of your superpower.

The next two chapters will help focus your attention on the moments from your past that will most likely point to your superpower.

Remember Your Mojo Moments

◆◆◆

Be the flow.
- Jay-Z

Mojo Moments are the highlight reel of your life experiences. They are the times in your life when you were at your very best. The times in your life when you felt completely alive and full of energy. The times when you were on your A-game. Times when you accomplished a lot with seemingly little effort. Times when you even exceeded your own expectations.

But it's more than just achieving positive outcomes. Mojo Moments are about joy. When we experience Mojo Moments, we often lose track of time, becoming completely immersed in the task at hand. People often refer to this as "flow." Most of us can recall a few of these moments from our past.

Recall a moment from your past when you were really on your game. Maybe it was a great day at work, or maybe it was something more personal. Just choose one moment and grab something to write on. We're going to do a five-minute exercise.

Once you've come up with your Mojo Moment, spend a minute or two remembering back to that day. Try to recall as much detail as you can about what you were doing, where you were, how you felt, who was around you, etc. Try to bring yourself back to that Mojo Moment in time.

Once you've spent a couple of minutes reliving the memory, ponder the questions below. Write down your responses so that you can refer back to them later. Don't worry about making your answers pretty. Spelling doesn't count. This is for your reference only. (NOTE: You can also download the Mojo Moments worksheet from the Digital Appendix.)

- How were you doing what you were doing? Remember, your superpower isn't about *what* you do, it's about *the way* you do it. Describe *the way* you were doing in as much detail as you can.
- What details mattered most to you? Where was the focus of your attention?
- What were the people around you doing? How was your contribution different from theirs?
- What about you allowed you to be successful in that situation?
- What if someone else had been in your place instead, what might they have done differently?
- What about your role and contribution makes you the proudest?

Once you've completed your reflection, walk away for a while. You can continue reading or come back to this book later. You just dug up some deep memories and we want to give your brain some time to simmer. You can even repeat this exercise a few more times, over the next few days, using different events from your past.

After you've given yourself some time away, go back and review what you wrote, looking for things that jump out at you. Circle any powerful phrases. Make note of any prominent themes. Notice the things that surprise you. The things that make you smile. All of these things serve breadcrumbs, leading to your superpower.

Hopefully you're getting a sense of how your Mojo Moments can be helpful for identifying where your superpower may lie. In the next section, I'll share my personal example of doing this Mojo Moments exercise. Back then, I didn't call them Mojo Moments, because I hadn't come up with that term yet. But as you'll see, that's exactly what they were.

My Mojo Moment, October 2014

I mentioned a while back that my superpower is serving as a *bridge between body and soul.* I remember the exact day these words came to me. I was deep in the Gila National Forest in New Mexico, four days into a five-day vision quest. I was alone, save for the occasional wild rabbit with whom I shared a steep and rocky mountainside. I was hungry, because I was fasting and hadn't eaten in more than 90 hours. And I was probably going a bit stir-crazy, given I didn't have my phone, iPad, or any other creature comforts of modern life. My only entertainment came from my notebook and a pen.

I was creating a list of all of the coaching clients I'd worked with over the past three years. I listed as many names as I could remember. I was pleased to see how many there were. Three years had flown by. I began thinking about the progress that each of these people had made in our time together. Of course, some made more progress than others. The most rewarding thing for a coach is having the chance to witness one of your clients make massive progress toward their goals.

A handful of names rose to the top of the list. The names of people whose lives had changed remarkably for the better during our time together. I began reflecting on the details of what each of these special people had been working on back then. Their challenges. Their goals. The outcomes they achieved. At first, I was just jotting down facts as they popped into my mind. Then slowly, I began adding my own words and ideas to the page. It became a creative endeavor. It became a spiritual endeavor. Eventually, I was no longer speaking to the pages, they were speaking to me.

At some point, I drew a picture of a bridge. On either side of the bridge I wrote the words "Body" and "Soul." It felt right. It felt true. It felt like home.

That day in 2014 wasn't the end of my superpower journey.

It was the beginning.

***

Additional Resources

Check out the **Mojo Moments**
worksheet in the Digital Appendix.

www.superpower50.com

Remember Your Oh No Moments

◆◆◆

The phoenix must burn to emerge.
- Janet Fitch, American author

We've all had moments where we stumbled. Where we failed to live up to our own expectations. Part of doing big things is knowing that sometimes we may come up short.

Are you the type of person who likes to move on from those moments and never look back at them? If so, you're missing a great opportunity to learn, but more specifically, to learn about your superpower. Although it may be painful to relive those lesser moments from your life, it will be worth the effort. Trust me. Are you willing to give it a shot?

Start by looking back over your life to find situations where you thought you were going to be successful, but you came up short. Perhaps you have some examples of projects that you took on with the best intentions, only to find yourself slogging through, or bailing out entirely. Perhaps you thought you were getting into one thing, only to find yourself deeply involved in something completely different, and not in a good way. Try to identify a few examples. The more significant, the better.

These are your **Oh No Moments**.

As you examine these Oh No Moments, look for patterns and common threads. Is there a particular task or type of activity that you were doing during these moments of stumble? Are there similarities about the circumstances that strike you as interesting? Is there something similar about the roles you were playing?

It's also helpful to examine these Oh No Moments against your Mojo Moments. What is different about the two lists? When it comes to this type of comparison, the subtle details can be very telling.

Consider this analogy. Imagine your best tool is a flathead screwdriver. You'll find yourself attracted to projects where a screwdriver is needed. But every once in a while, you'll encounter a Phillips screw. You can probably use your flathead screwdriver to do the job, but your results may not be as good. Your work may not be as clean. Noticing the subtle difference between the exact tool for the job and a tool that is merely adequate might be tough, unless you are paying close attention.

Now apply that same concept to discovering your superpower. The devil is in the details. In some ways, superpower is very subtle. Noticing where your superpower doesn't quite work can be as informative as noticing the times when it works perfectly.

Let's do a similar exercise to the one in the previous chapter. Identify an Oh No Moment from your past. Maybe a time when you started something brimming with enthusiasm and confidence, only to find yourself way off track and way out of your comfort zone. Take a couple of minutes to take yourself back to that fateful day. Then use these questions to structure your reflection:

- How did you get into the situation? What was the sequence of events?
- At what point did you go from feeling comfortable to feeling less comfortable?
- How did your role or contribution change in that exact moment?
- How might someone else have been better suited to play your role in that moment?
- How did that experience alter your future behavior?

Once again, give your subconscious brain some time to ponder these reflections. Walk away. Come back later. Do this exercise again. Compare your results. Look for patterns. Compare your Oh No Moments with your Mojo Moments and see if anything pops out at you.

I hope the last two chapters have demonstrated that our past can be nearly as revealing as our present when it comes to superpower discovery. Is there any place else to look? Yep. There's one more place. Buckle up. We're going there.

***

Additional Resources

Check out the **Oh No Moments** worksheet in the Digital Appendix.

www.superpower50.com

Listen to the Future

◆◆◆

The future influences the present.
- Friedrich Nietzsche

Believe it or not, you can learn a lot about your superpower from events yet to come.

I'm not suggesting you run to the nearest psychic or consult the local paper for your horoscope. There's nothing magical or mystical about this. At least there needn't be. There's a perfectly rational explanation for why we can predict the future.

It doesn't matter how long we've been living the Clark Kent life, telling the world that we don't have a superpower. On some level, each of us has an intuitive sense of our unique ability.

You have a lifetime of experiences. Challenges met and overcome. In some of those cases, even if you didn't realize it, you used your superpower. Maybe it was only for an instant, but you did. These moments are seared into your brain. Your superpower memories may be buried deep, but they exist. Trust me.

Part of you knows.

Listen to the Whispers

Don't expect your subconscious to scream for attention. Our subconscious voice doesn't scream. It whispers. It speaks to us in hushed tones, when our mind is already quiet. Our subconscious generates deep and subtle longings for something different in our lives.

Is there a job or a project you've always felt drawn toward? Some people might say they have a "calling." Do you have a calling that you've been reluctant to answer? If so, this might be your superpower seeking a channel to express itself.

Maybe there is a particular person. Someone you've always found curious and attractive. Not in a romantic way, but almost a subtle admiration. It's possible you see something in them that reminds you of your superpower.

Do you find yourself attracted to particular types of situations? You sense what is going on and part of you knows … *that is my work.* What is that work? Who are the people you would be serving? What superpower makes sense in light of the answers to these questions?

Listening to the whispers from the future is tricky business. Most of us prefer big and bold, like a billboard telling us exactly what to do. Our subconscious prefers a subtler approach. It nudges us toward certain situations and experiences but leaves the final decision up to our conscious brain. What is "intuition" if not the hand-off between our subconscious mind and our conscious mind?

Spend some time listening to your intuition. Spend some time listening to the whispers. You might be pleased to hear what they tell you.

The next two chapters will discuss some techniques for allowing the whispers to come forward.

Get Your Hands Dirty

◆◆◆

Observation is a passive science,
experimentation an active science.
- Claude Bernard

How do you tap into the wisdom of the future when the
future isn't here yet? You have to bring the future to you.
It's not enough to simply imagine a future where your
superpower is fully functional, front and center, in your
life. In order bring the future to you, you need to get out of
your head and get into action. Here are a few ways to do
this, without disrupting everything else in your life.

Conduct Some Interviews

Is there someone you really admire? It could be someone
close to you, but it could even be someone you've never
met. What about that person attracts you? In movies and
books, the hero always finds a mentor who helps them
discover their true potential. We're attracted to people we
believe might be good mentors. It's possible that your
superpower might be part of that attraction. Your
subconscious might be telling you … *That's someone we need
to talk to.*

Can you arrange to have a conversation with that person?
Ask them about the secret to their success. What makes
them tick? Ask them what they think makes them different
from other people. Ask them … *What's your superpower?*

As you talk to this person, listen to their answers deeply.
On multiple levels. Listen to the words, of course, but

listen for the passion and the emotion. Listen for the phrases that jump out at you, either because the person uses them over and over again, or because they use them in a way that you've never heard before. Feel how their words are ever so slightly different from the words that you might choose for yourself. That's where you'll find your superpower.

What happens if you admire someone who's famous and inaccessible to you? Tony Robbins. Oprah Winfrey. Warren Buffet. These aren't people you'll likely bump into at the local coffee shop. What are your options then?

If the person has written an autobiography, read it. Even if it's not an autobiography, but the person has written a book, they'll often give you some insights into their superpower, even if they never use that word. Personally, I get more from hearing someone speak than I get from reading their words. Look for interviews on Youtube. Podcasts. Find those rare moments when the person was being completely open and honest about themselves and maybe you'll find some gold.

You can learn a lot from the people you admire most.

Design an Experiment

When it comes to superpower discovery, nothing beats real-time feedback. Designing an experiment that provides real-life, real-time feedback is a great option.

What does a superpower discovery experiment look like? It's really anything that puts you into a situation where you can DO things in a relatively low-risk environment, so that you can watch for the emergence of your superpower.

This technique works well if you have a sense of the general area where your superpower might reside, but you just can't nail down the details. For example, if you think your superpower might have something to do with teaching, maybe you can volunteer to teach a class at a local social center. If you think your superpower might have something to do with empathy, maybe you can visit a nursing home or a prison. If you think your superpower has something to do with connection, maybe you could write essays for children and read them aloud in classrooms.

These days, there are so many different options available to us. Is there an online course related to the subject matter? Is there a hobby that would allow you to get a taste of a particular area of interest? Are there meetup groups in your area where other people are coming together to explore common interests? Is there a working group or a committee within your current place of employment that will give you exposure to new areas or ways of working?

Don't look at these ideas as definitive solutions to discovering your superpower. Instead, think of them as a series of doors leading to rooms of mystery and surprise. Maybe as you experiment with reading essays for young children you discover that your "connection" is stronger with older kids, which leads you to working with teenagers instead. How can you ever make this discovery if you don't conduct the first experiment? You can't.

By putting yourself into new situations and then paying close attention to how you experience those situations, you'll create opportunities for your superpower to emerge.

Disturb the System

◆◆◆

Comfort zones are plush lined coffins.
When you stay in your plush lined coffins, you die.
- Stan Dale

Life By Default is the enemy of superpower discovery. If you continue to live and think in the same patterns, all day, every day, it's really hard to notice something extraordinary about yourself. Until now, we've been trying to break the habitual patterns of your thinking. This might not be enough for you. We may need to go further. We may need to really shake things up so we can liberate your mind from the constraints that are holding you back.

I mentioned earlier that my superpower came to me during a vision quest in the Gila National Forest. A vision quest is an example of something that I call a **Designed Disturbance**. In my case, the disturbance included five days of fasting, in total solitude, while immersed in nature. This is the classic vision quest formula that people have been using for thousands of years.

What is so special about this formula that has allowed it to endure for millennia? It breaks just about every structure and pattern of normal, everyday life. Without meals, you lose a significant amount of your daily structure, not to mention the mental and physical effects of hunger. Without other people around, you're left alone with your own thoughts. In nature, you don't have a couch, or a television, a toilet, or a roof. Everything that you've come to rely upon for normalcy is gone.

It's in this absence of familiarity that novelty emerges.

We spend so much of our lives following familiar patterns and rules that sometimes we need to design a disturbance to our system so that we can be free of those constraints. So that we can see the world in a new way.

You don't need to do a vision quest to find your superpower. When it comes to a vision quest, having a very specific outcome in mind, such as discovering your superpower, probably isn't going to work anyway. More than likely, you'll get in your own way. Grasping doesn't work. The secret is in *not* grasping. It's the disruption that allows insights to emerge.

Also, your designed disturbance doesn't need to be so extreme. Most of us can benefit from a simple break from our normal pattern. A break that includes time and space to think. Time and space to allow the wisdom that's already inside of us to emerge.

Ditch the smartphone. Turn off the computer. Pretend email was never invented. Grab a notebook and a pen. Go for a walk in the woods. Get closer to nature. Take a day or even a weekend and spend some quality time with the *one* person who knows your superpower better than anyone.

Yeah. I'm talking about you.

From Zero to 1.0

◆◆◆

In the movies, the hero discovers their superpower in a single moment of epiphany. In real life, it doesn't work this way. Discovering our superpower is an iterative process. It takes time. It takes work. It involves trial and it definitely involves error.

If you've done the work of *Getting to 1.0*, you should be ready to get over that first barrier. Feeling nervous? Don't be. There's no pressure. Remember, we're not trying to get it right. Give yourself permission to stumble. Permission to learn. Permission to absolutely make s#!t up. Do it now.

I think there's a chance that my superpower is related to…

_____

_____

There you go. You've taken the first step. You now have version 1.0 of your superpower. Did you get it right? No chance. Does it matter? Not one bit.

Superpower version 1.0 is infinitely better than version zero.

Getting to 2.0

◆◆◆

By now, you've come up with your superpower, version 1.0. In other words, you are able to complete this sentence:

I think there's a chance that my superpower is …

_____

_____

Don't worry if you don't feel totally comfortable with your answer. You shouldn't. In fact, at this point, you should be feeling a little bit uncomfortable. If you're not, then you probably need to slow down a bit. Allow me to explain.

I meet a lot of people who already have a sense of their superpower. Sometimes they can even describe their superpower, clearly and succinctly. This may seem like a good thing, but I find it often causes the person to miss an opportunity. Great designers know the best time to revise and refine is in the early stages. The closer you get to a final product, the more difficult it is to make changes.

When it comes to superpower design, the early stages offer the opportunity to make revisions and upgrades because you have not yet formed a strong attachment to any particular wording or understanding. At this stage, language matters. The words you choose to name your superpower make all the difference between a kick-ass superpower and one that is just okay.

Getting to 2.0 is all about helping you make that difference. Getting to superpower version 2.0 means answering the question:

How can I design my superpower into something that inspires me to action?

Make it Pop

◆◆◆

The secret of being boring is to say everything.
- Voltaire

Take a look at your superpower version 1.0. How does it make you feel when you read the words? Where does it hit you? Does it make you smile? Does it cause your stomach to tighten? Does it make you want to stand up and move? Stand up and dance?

On a scale from 1-10, how juicy is your superpower? Does it really pop when you say it?

Does your superpower simultaneously inspire and scare you? Does it fill you with curiosity and wonder? Does it make you to want to *do* something, right now?

When I think of my superpower—*a bridge between body and soul*—my energy swells and I actually get a bit anxious. Life starts to feel urgent. I need to be in motion. I need to do my work.

My superpower is juicy. It's compelling. It's a 10 for me. It pops.

If yours is anything less than an 8, we've got work to do. Fear not. It's a process. Let's keep going.

Your Words Matter

I'm a bit of a word nerd. A stickler for language. I love finding the absolute right word for every situation. I'm all about potency. Vivid imagery. The perfect words stir the soul. Don't believe me?

Check out this passage from Cormac McCarthy's *All the Pretty Horses*. I came across this in the mid-90's and it has stuck with me ever since. In this scene, John Grady Cole's father is riding behind his son when he notices something he'd never noticed before.

> "The boy who rode on slightly before him sat a horse not only as if he'd been born to it which he was but as if were he begot by malice or mischance into some queer land where horses never were he would have found them anyway. Would have known that there was something missing for the world to be right or he right in it and would have set forth to wander wherever it was needed for as long as it took until he came upon one and he would have known that that was what he sought and it would have been." (McCarthy, 1993)

Talk about juicy. That's a 10 in my book. Not in a million years could I have come up with that. I probably would have said something like "The boy was a natural. His father had never seen anyone so comfortable on a horse." That's a 4, at best.

But McCarthy is a master of language and he uses it to give the reader an image that is utterly undeniable. We read this paragraph and we know that John Grady Cole doesn't just love horses and they don't just love him. We read this paragraph and we know that horses are a piece of John Grady Cole's soul. They are essential to his very being. *Damn.*

That's what we're after when we name your superpower. I'm guessing you are not a Pulitzer Prize-winning author, but that doesn't mean you shouldn't strive for some seriously powerful prose.

Remember, your superpower is unique. Mere words will never completely capture that, but you should try. The more dynamic your language, the more unique your superpower becomes. The more compelling and provocative it becomes for you and for everyone around you.

Upgrade from Plain to Potent

Usually when people first name their superpower, they land on plain language. This isn't a bad thing, because at least it gets the ball rolling. The problem with plain language is that it doesn't do much to differentiate. Differentiation is where the magic lies. Our goal is to find words that feel unique to your *way* of being in the world. We want words that pack a punch.

I hesitate to provide too many specific examples, because I worry about over-influencing your discovery process. But in this case, I think it's worth the risk to show you what I mean by upgrading your language. Below are examples of how a few people upgraded their superpower language.

Started with ... *I'm incredibly honest.* Upgraded to ... *Bringing voice to the truth.*

Started with ... *I'm empathetic.* Upgraded to ... *I invite people to be seen.*

Started with … *I'm good at managing complex projects*.
Upgraded to … *I see the entire field*.

Started with … *I'm a teacher*. Upgraded to … *I'm a bridge between body and soul*.

Can you feel the difference between the original superpower and the upgraded language? And that's just from your outside perspective. Imagine how much more powerful it was for each of these people. The real power and differentiation will reside in your mind. You will be the primary beneficiary of the potent language.

There's something else I'd like to point out to you. Take another look at those examples. In some cases, the person chose more dynamic words to describe the same concept. But some of the examples go much further. The upgraded language is almost unrecognizable in comparison to the starting point. Sometimes your initial language merely points to a concept that you need to explore deeper.

Where can you go to find more potent and powerful words? How can you determine if the words you are choosing are simply pointing to a concept, beneath which lies your superpower? The next three chapters will give you the tools you'll need to dig deeper so you can find the gold beneath the surface.

Tell Your Story

◆◆◆

Story, as it turns out, was crucial to our evolution—more so than opposable thumbs. Opposable thumbs let us hang on; story told us what to hang on to.
- Lisa Cron, author of *Wired for Story*

You don't need a thesaurus to find substitutes for the words you've already written down. You need to find the truth that lies beneath those words. The way to do this is by telling stories. Telling your story, even telling it to yourself, is powerful. When you tell a personal story, you tap into an inner truth. An inner knowing. You don't have to *think* about the words, they'll just come.

These words are magical. This is where you'll find the potency and the power.

If you can, find a partner. Explain that you're working on designing your superpower and you can really use their help. All they have to do is listen to you and then tell you what they heard. All you have to do is tell them a story.

Tell your partner a story about your superpower. Make it a real story. Don't talk in abstract terms. As you are telling your story, the word "superpower" should never come up. You didn't have that word in your vocabulary back when the story took place, right? Just simply tell the person what happened, as it happened.

What was the situation? What was your role? What emotions were you feeling? What challenge did you overcome and how did you overcome it? What felt most important to you at the time? Did you notice anything different about yourself from the other people who were involved? Was there something in particular that you did, or realized, that made all the difference in that situation?

These questions are just ideas to get you going. There's really no set of "right" questions to ask yourself. Just tell the story with as much detail as you can, as if you were painting a picture for the other person. Tell it as if you are reliving the moment right now.

After you've told your story, ask the person what they heard. Ask them to identify any words that you used over and over again. Did they notice any unique phrases? Where did they hear excitement and passion in your voice? Ask your partner if they have any questions about your story. What do they find most interesting? Then get interested in what they find interesting.

A Word of Warning

Finding skillful conversation partners isn't always easy. Some people are really good at listening and asking thoughtful questions. Other people get too caught up in the details to really offer any meta-level insights. Some people will find the work you are doing quite fascinating and they'll be eager to help. Others will find this kind of work strange and they may not feel comfortable having this kind of conversation. Simply try to meet people wherever they are. Keep an open mind and be curious to see what happens. This is part of the fun!

If there's absolutely no way for you to work with a partner, I recommend having a conversation with an imaginary partner, while recording your voice. This will likely feel incredibly strange at first. Just remind yourself that nobody but you will ever hear the recording. Don't rehearse and don't write your story out beforehand. You wouldn't do that for a chat with a friend. Simply talk. Allow your thoughts to flow. Then go back after some time has passed and listen to the recording.

***

Additional Resources

Check out the **Storytelling 101** worksheet in the Digital Appendix.

www.superpower50.com

Take it for a Test Drive

◆◆◆

If it's not broken, tinker with it till
you find out how it works.
- Bob Proctor, American author

Now that you've practiced telling your superpower story, it's time to take this baby out for a test drive. We need to see how your superpower handles in the real world.

The first step is to keep your superpower in your awareness throughout the day. Grab yourself some sticky notes, write your superpower on each one, and then strategically place them around as reminders. Most days, I have one hanging off the edge of my computer monitor and one stuck to the inside of my notebook. In the past, I've changed the screensaver on all my devices to be a superpower-reminder. By reminding yourself of your superpower throughout the day, your brain will automatically begin analyzing it for accuracy.

When you feel comfortable, start to invite other people into your test drive. Consider changing your email signature to include a declaration of your superpower. This will do two things. Not only will it be your first public declaration of your superpower, but it will also be a great conversation starter.

Starting conversations is one of our goals at this point. The more people you can tell, the more conversations you can have, the more opportunity you have to refine and reaffirm your superpower.

The Initial Awkwardness

In the beginning, you may feel uncomfortable talking about your superpower with people. I'll admit, it's a bit unusual. Most people don't walk around town talking about "superpowers." Of course, there's no rule that says you have to use that word. Especially in the beginning, you may choose more common language, calling it "your greatest strength" or "your unique gift" or "your forehand" if you're into sports analogies. It's up to you, but I think you'll be surprised how many people are on board with calling it a "superpower."

One of the easiest ways to break through the awkwardness is to blame me. Literally. Tell people you've been reading this crazy book that encourages people to discover their superpower and you'd like to get some opinions on what you've come up with so far.

Notice Their Reaction

There's tremendous value in getting an outside perspective. The way other people experience us is not always congruent with the way we see ourselves or the way we imagine other people see us. You may think your superpower is one thing, but the people around you experience it a different way. Which one is right? Who's to say? Remember, you're not seeking approval, per se, but you are looking for information. How a particular person reacts when you tell them your superpower is useful information. You then need to decide what to do with that information.

As you share your superpower with other people, it's important to remember that superpower design is an iterative process. Each interaction with another person is a mini experiment, the results of which allow us to make useful adjustments. There's no such thing as failure. There's only new information.

Warning! Naysayers Ahead

You should be prepared for a bit of disappointment when you share your superpower with other people. The fact that you are reading this book, the fact that you are interested in discovering and cultivating your superpower, indicates something very important about you. You are **Living By Design**. Most people are not.

Most people are **Living By Default**. They are just going through the motions. They don't spend a single minute thinking about their life, let alone their superpower. The fact that you are doing this kind of work may stir up unsettling feelings about the way they are living their own life. This might cause them to resist your ideas. Don't be discouraged. It doesn't mean you're missing the mark.

Keep in mind, we don't see the world as it is, we see the world as we are. That means when people look at you, they see you through their own eyes. Through their own lenses and filters. Their interpretation will never match yours. Not exactly. And that's okay.

Although it is useful to get input from the people around you about your superpower, the words you choose are, first and foremost, for you. I recommend using the thoughts and ideas from the people around you as an input, but ultimately, the decision of how to name your superpower is your decision.

Notice How it Feels

How does it feel when you name your superpower to other people? How did it feel when you thought about adding your superpower to your email signature?

Something very subtle and very interesting happens when you tell someone else about your superpower. You make the shift from **naming** to **claiming**. When you claim, you take ownership. That superpower is yours. It's a huge move.

Notice that feeling.

Does it feel right? Does it feel solid? Does it feel true? Does it make you proud to hear yourself say the words? To own them? Notice the difference between the way you feel about making your claim and the way you feel about the reaction you get. That's the feeling of unique. That's where your superpower lives.

Never Stop Tinkering

Practice telling your story and then watching people's reactions. Pay attention to your own reactions. As you do, make adjustments. Continue to refine your language. A tweak here. An upgrade there. Don't be afraid to make changes. If you make a change and it doesn't work, simply change it back. It's that easy.

Just like the quote at the beginning of this chapter, the goal is to develop a deeper understanding. Naming your superpower is not a matter of right versus wrong. Your superpower is right regardless of whether you know what to call it. But having the right words helps you to better understand this remarkable gift that you have. This remarkable gift that you are.

Figure Out What It's Not

◆◆◆

I saw the angel in the marble and carved until I set him free.
- Michelangelo

When someone commented on how challenging it must have been to carve the statue of *David*, Michelangelo said, "It was easy. I just chipped away the stone that didn't look like David."

Up until now, we've been focused on trying to pinpoint what your superpower *is*, but it's just as important to recognize what your superpower is not. To do this, we're going to the **Superpower Rings** diagram:

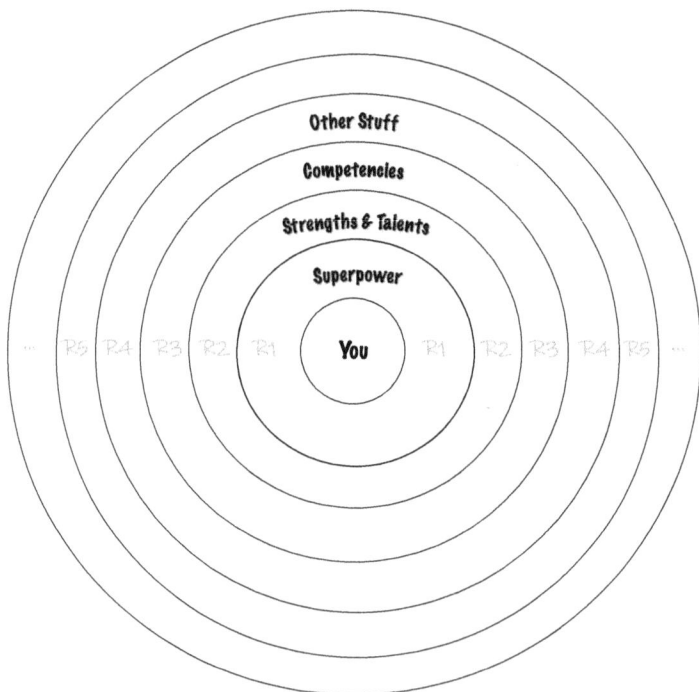

The rings work like a map and will help you identify and appreciate the full terrain of your life. On this map, you are at the center and everything emanates from you. As you move outward, you move farther and farther from your energetic center. The ring that is closest to you is your superpower (R1). The rings that are closest to your superpower are the areas of the highest energy, passion, and competence. Each subsequent ring represents parts of your life that are further and further removed from your superpower.

The second ring (R2) is labeled "Strengths and Talents." These are things that you are really, really good at doing. In fact, the people around you might mistake things in ring #2 as your superpower. The second ring can be tricky to define because your strengths and talents are often closely related to your superpower. At a glance, they may appear identical, but they are not exactly the same. You can learn a lot from the subtle nuance between your superpower and your other talents. Before you named your superpower, you could not have noticed this level of granularity and distinction.

The third ring (R3), which lies beyond your strengths and talents, is labeled "Competencies." These are areas of your life where you've developed adequate skills, but not so much that you'd call them a talent. You can get by, but maybe you don't excel in these areas. Once again, you may find competencies that are closely related to your talents or even to your superpower, but at the same time, these areas will be distinctly different.

The circles extend infinitely. In fact, beyond your superpower ring, the labels are not set in stone. You can call them whatever you prefer. I labeled them as you see above merely for illustrative purposes. The most important thing is to recognize how the rings differ from one another. The activities that fall in ring #2 will be slightly less energizing and you'll have slightly less competency in those areas when compared to your superpower. Things in ring #3 will be slightly less than ring #2 and so on.

Here is an example to help illustrate how the rings work.

Noticing Subtle Differences - Meet Janet

Janet is a senior executive at a consulting firm. Her superpower is: *Overcoming any obstacle.* This superpower has served Janet well throughout her consulting career and has led to her tremendous professional success.

As part of her superpower design process, Janet began mapping other aspects of her work onto the superpower rings. She quickly identified one of her strengths and talents (ring #2) is: *Helping other people to overcome their challenges.*

Notice the similarity between Janet's superpower and her talent. They are quite similar, but if you look closely, you will see they are substantially different. Janet's superpower is overcoming her own obstacles, but she's also quite talented at helping other people to overcome their obstacles.

This might not seem like a huge difference to you, but to Janet, the distinction is crucial. Janet is at her best when she's operating from her superpower ring. Although she's incredibly talented when she's working in ring #2, it's slightly off her sweet spot.

As such, when Janet decides to take on commitments that involve helping other people overcome their obstacles, she recognizes this is likely going to require more of her energy and more of her attention. Janet is still free to take on tasks and projects that fall outside of her superpower, and even ones that fall outside of her strengths and talents, but she's able to do so with more intention.

The superpower rings helped Janet become more explicit not only about what her superpower is, but about what her superpower is not. This serves to deepen Janet's appreciation of her superpower, but also for the broader landscape of her life.

Perform a Differential Diagnosis

Doctors use a process called a **differential diagnosis** to determine what might be causing a patient's symptoms. The doctors list all of the symptoms, then list all of the diseases that might cause them. They go through and eliminate potential causes, one by one, until they are left with the most likely candidate for what is causing the problem.

One of the most powerful ways to discover the true nature of your superpower is by doing a similar process on your own life. Start examining all of the things that you do. Areas where you spend big chunks of your time. The types of projects you typically take on and the tasks that you wind up doing within these projects.

Keep in mind, you're not trying to map every single thing you do in your life, although, theoretically you could map every single thing onto the superpower rings. At this stage, your goal is to develop a deeper appreciation for your superpower by noticing what it is not. That means identifying things that are similar to what you think your superpower is. Then you can compare and contrast the subtlest details. Ask yourself these questions:

- Which one feels the strongest in terms of my competency?
- Which one feels like it comes first, chronologically?
- Is one "cause" and the other "effect"?
- Which one feels more like the real you, if you drop away all of the constraints and circumstances?

If you've ever had an eye exam for glasses, you've done the test where the doctor has you look through two lenses and you say which one is clearer. Keep comparing things until your superpower becomes super-clear. You might be surprised by what you see.

In the early stages of superpower discovery, you may find that something you thought was your superpower actually belongs in ring #2 and that you've identified something even better for your superpower. Be open to this changing. It's more important to get it right than it is to have been right all along.

**

Additional Resources

Check out the **Superpower Rings** Diagram in the Digital Appendix.

www.superpower50.com

From 1.0 to 2.0

◆◆◆

For many, the hardest part about superpower design is going from zero to 1.0. For most people, the most exhilarating part is going from 1.0 to 2.0. This is where you take the plain, generic language that makes your superpower sound similar to everyone else's and you turn up the gas.

Your version 2.0 superpower should energize you. It should make you want to get out of your chair and go do something in the world. Your superpower 2.0 language should feel both potent and precise. It should feel completely your own.

So, what is your superpower?

My superpower is…

_____

_____

On a scale from 1-10, how juicy is it?

If it's at least a 7, then you've done enough for now. You can always refine your language down the road. If you're still not feeling it, I recommend circling back to some of the earlier exercises. Maybe you need to walk away from this work for a little while and let your subconscious mind settle what you've stirred up.

The point is, you probably don't want to go too much further without feeling pretty good about your version 2.0, because it's about to get real.

Getting to 3.0

◆◆◆

Congratulations! You've completed the first two stages of the superpower design process. It may not feel like much, but trust me, the foundation that you've laid for yourself will support you throughout the rest of your journey.

Let's quickly recap how we got here.

The chances are, you came to the party with at least some level of curiosity and optimism. There are a lot of people in the world who live in total denial of the very notion they have a superpower. Those people don't read books like this one. You're different. Perhaps you started out skeptical, but you overcame that initial hesitation. You made the move from zero to one.

Superpower version 1.0 is really about answering one question: What is my superpower? You've examined your life, past, present, and future to identify the *way* you do what you do, that is uniquely you.

Then we began working on your superpower, version 2.0. The difference between version 1.0 and version 2.0 is a matter of refinement. We fine-tuned the language. We solicited input from the people around you and then we fine-tuned the language even further. We paid attention, not only to notice what your superpower is, but to notice what it is not. All of this effort, with a single question in mind: How can I design my superpower into something that energizes and inspires me?

Once you've answered that question, you are ready to move into the next phase of superpower design. In *Getting to 3.0*, our goal is to answer this question:

How can I make my superpower work for me?

Application is Everything

◆◆◆

Knowing is not enough, we must apply.
Willing is not enough, we must do.
- Bruce Lee

Imagine if Superman never donned his cape. Imagine if he spent his entire life living as Clark Kent. He might use his superhuman strength to get the top off of a jar every now and again. He might choose to fly to the office rather than sit in morning traffic, but it wouldn't be the same. He wouldn't be Superman.

This is what it's like to have superpower version 2.0. You recognize that you have this superpower and you're excited about it. You might even find opportunities to use it from time to time; Though, probably not as often as you'd like. And the times when you do use your superpower, it's almost as likely to be an accident as it is to be an intentional, thoughtful application.

We've arrived at the stage where you have to wrestle with some challenging questions. You have this unique gift. Your superpower. You are the only one who has it. What are you doing with it? What is it doing for you? What is your superpower doing for the rest of us?

It's not enough to *have* a superpower. You have to *use* it. You're obligated to use it. I'm not talking about using it every once in a while. I'm not talking about the times when your superpower kicks in automatically and you don't even realize it's happening. I'm talking about learning to use your superpower with full intention.

What is intention?

INTENTION = AWARENESS + PURPOSE

You want to be purposeful with your superpower. You owe it to yourself. You owe it to your family. You owe it to the world. Deep down, you know this is true.

But the distance between knowing and doing is massive.

Now it's time to put your superpower to work.

Make no mistake, it will be work. Until now, this has largely been a thought experiment. An exercise of the mind. This is where it gets real.

Active vs. Passive

◆◆◆

Awareness is the greatest agent for change.
- Eckhart Tolle

What did Superman always do immediately before he launched into action? He ducked into the nearest phone booth for a quick wardrobe change. He put on his cape. Superman was intentional about using his superpower.

Before you use your superpower, do you consciously ask yourself if your superpower is needed? Probably not.

More than likely, you just launch right in. Your superpower just happens. You might not even realize it until after the fact, when you look back and notice "Oh, yeah. That was my superpower back there."

This is called superpower **passive mode** and it has some serious limitations. There's a old saying "when your favorite tool is a hammer, everything looks like a nail." This describes perfectly what happens to us in superpower passive mode.

See if this feels familiar…

You have a superpower and you know it works really well, so you start using it more often. Next thing you know, you're using it for everything. The problem is, sometimes your superpower is the right tool for the job but sometimes it's not. Sometimes your superpower is the exact wrong tool for the job.

Even if your superpower is the right tool for the job, in passive mode, you'll lack the awareness needed to calibrate your superpower intensity. If you ever watched the *Incredible Hulk* television series, you know what I mean. The Hulk couldn't control his strength very well. He always got the job done, but there was usually a pile of broken furniture in his wake. He was a wrecking ball. The Hulk lacked precision.

An uncalibrated superpower is the Hulk in a china shop.

Why bring level-10 intensity to a situation when a 5 or 6 would suffice? Maybe a 5 or 6 would be even better.

Switch into Active Mode

Superpower **active mode** means you are conscious of the situation at hand. You decide whether or not your superpower is the right tool for the job. If the situation warrants using your superpower, you determine the appropriate intensity, *before* you act. You closely monitor the results that you are getting, and adjust accordingly.

In active mode, you are aware and purposeful.

The next three chapters explore some different ways that you can actively use your superpower.

***

Additional Resources

Check out the **Active Awareness** practice in the Digital Appendix.

www.superpower50.com

To Tackle a Specific Challenge

◆◆◆

Being good is something that you must choose over and over again, every day, throughout the day, for the rest of your life.
- Cate Tiernan, author

We face challenges every day. Some small. Some significant. Every decision is, on some level, a challenge. This isn't news. It's always been this way. Now you have the added dimension of your superpower. For many of the challenges that you face each day, your superpower will be the perfect tool for the job.

When it comes to applying your superpower to specific challenges, the work isn't in the application of your superpower, the work is in deciding whether or not to apply your superpower in the first place.

Before you act, stop and ask yourself "Will my superpower be useful in this situation?"

Warning! In the early days of superpower development, most of us suffer from one of two afflictions. Either we think that our superpower is right for every situation or we don't think it's right for any situation. Identifying which one best describes you is like taking a superpower Rorschach test. Are you prone to overuse or underuse?

I'd like to share another example, because it illustrates how difficult it sometimes be to decide whether or not to use your superpower.

To Use or Not to Use - Meet Marc

Marc is a professional life coach and executive coach. His superpower is: *I see behind the mask.*

Marc has a unique ability to see past any facades that a person might be hiding behind and to see their underlying truth. His superpower stems from his essential humility and vulnerability, which help to create connection and trust with everyone he meets. As you can probably imagine, this is a very useful superpower for a coach.

At the same time, Marc has come to realize that using his superpower isn't always appropriate. There's a time and a place for everything. Sometimes people aren't ready to be seen. After all, they are wearing their mask for a reason.

Through his work with the superpower design process, Marc realized that even though he always has good intentions, his superpower has the potential to make someone feel uncomfortable if they are not prepared to be seen in such a deep and powerful way.

In order to prevent this from happening, Marc must be intentional about calibrating his superpower to match the moment. Marc is careful to wait for an invitation before turning his superpower up to high intensity. If he doesn't receive an invitation, Marc dials his superpower way back, almost to zero.

Sometimes this is easier said than done. Marc's superpower is part of him. It's deep in his core, so it often takes more effort to dial back his superpower than it would to let it run at full blast.

Your Day to Day Work

Once you've done the work of naming and claiming your superpower, your work changes. Now your work is deciding when, and with what intensity, to use your superpower. This requires you to hit "pause" and really assess each situation as it presents itself.

Is my superpower the right tool for this job? If so, what level of intensity will work best? How should I proceed? These are the questions you'll need to wrestle with each and every day.

How will you know the right answers? You won't. You can't know for sure.

That doesn't mean you shouldn't pause and ask the questions. The value is in the ask, not in the answer. Your intuition, your inner wisdom, is enough to guide you. But in order for that intuition and wisdom to come forward, you have to create space.

Pausing and asking the questions creates that space.

To Prioritize

◆◆◆

*Half of the troubles of this life can be traced to saying yes
too quickly and not saying no soon enough.*
- Josh Billings, 19th century American humorist

Whenever someone tells me they have a time management
problem, I tell them they have it wrong. We don't manage
time. We don't choose the number of hours in a day. We
choose how to spend them. We manage priorities.
Whenever someone believes they have a time management
problem, what they actually have is a prioritization
problem.

Your superpower can help you decide where to spend
your time and energy.

Superpower Prioritization - Meet Andrea

Andrea is a small business owner, mother of four, and a
social maven. Andrea is one of the busiest people you will
ever meet. Every entrepreneur knows, owning a small
business is enough to tip the work-life balance scales in the
wrong direction. Add four energetic children to the mix
and you've got a real situation on your hands.

Andrea's superpower is: *Fueled by enthusiasm.*

When she's excited about a particular project, Andrea is a
force of nature. And her enthusiasm is contagious, which is
why people love working with her. Who wouldn't want a
constant source of energy and optimism in their life?

The problem, as Andrea discovered, is that not all projects sustain her enthusiasm. Sometimes her excitement for a particular project runs out. When it does, her personal energy level drops and her attention wanders. This is Andrea's indication that it's time to move on to a new project that will spark her enthusiasm once again.

But sometimes this isn't easy. What if she's made a long-term commitment to a project? What if quitting isn't an option? Andrea can't just abandon every project once her enthusiasm wanes. That would be irresponsible, and she knows this. But knowing it doesn't mean always having the awareness to manage all of her commitments.

Things changed for Andrea when she discovered that her superpower centers around "enthusiasm." Now Andrea pays close attention to her enthusiasm. She's more attuned to the types of things that will sustain her enthusiasm long-term and the types of things that will most likely fade quickly. This awareness allows Andrea to be more careful about making long-term commitments to her friends and colleagues. It's also given Andrea a new model for managing her commitments. Now Andrea tries to to arrange her work in bursts and sprints, rather than marathons. When she is at her best, Andrea actively *uses* her superpower to help prioritize her commitments.

Your 24 Hours

There are only 24 hours in the day. You have limited resources when it comes to your time and your attention. Wouldn't it be amazing if you could take on tasks and responsibilities only when they are right in your superpower wheelhouse? Of course, you don't have that luxury. Nobody does.

But you can be more selective. Why not consider your superpower when making decisions about where to invest and commit your precious time and energy?

To Navigate

If you do not change direction,
you may end up where you are heading.
- Lao Tzu

I remember the first time I ever tried to navigate by compass. My wilderness survival instructor had just given me a 30-minute lesson and I was feeling confident. He said, "Meet me at the top of that mountain in two hours." *No problem*, I thought. *How hard can it be?* About an hour later, I understood exactly how hard it was. I was wandering in circles wondering where I'd gone wrong.

Our brains prefer to know exactly where we are going. Ubiquitous GPS devices, and their turn-by-turn directions, reinforce this subtle, subconscious desire. The idea of navigating by approximation, the way one must with a compass, is utterly foreign to most of us. It makes us uncomfortable, so we avoid it.

We operate the same way in our Life Design. Most of us spend a lot of time engaged in short-term thinking and problem-solving, but not a lot of time thinking about long-term strategy and direction. Long-term thinking is abstract. It's difficult to see how the parts add up to the whole. Long-term thinking is uncomfortable. So we avoid it.

This is where your superpower can help. Your superpower is a source of strength, energy, and potential. What if you found ways to use your superpower every single day? How might the trajectory of your life change? Of course, there's no way to know exactly where you would end up, but I bet it's someplace worthwhile.

It's one thing to use your superpower to affect specific situations and solve specific problems as they arise, but the real benefits come when you incorporate your superpower into your primary life systems. Solve a problem and you impact that specific area. Upgrade one of your life systems and the benefits are amplified over time. Systems, by their very nature, provide leverage. What do I mean by a life system?

How did you choose your job? How did you choose where to live? How do you choose which social groups to join and your role within them? These are life system decisions with long-term implications. To what extent was your superpower a factor in those decisions? What might you choose differently if you knew then what you know now about your superpower?

It's possible that your life is already organized around your superpower. For many people, this happens naturally. Perhaps you've gravitated to a career that rewards a superpower like yours. Perhaps you've chosen to partner with people who appreciate your superpower. Maybe you've chosen partners with superpowers that compliment your own. It often works out this way, by default.

But why leave it to chance? Why not be intentional? Why not actively and consciously use your superpower as a factor when making decisions about your most crucial life systems?

From 2.0 to 3.0

◆◆◆

In theory, there is no difference between theory and practice.
But in practice, there is.
- Benjamin Brewster

Don't treat superpower as an intellectual exercise. This isn't something that you think about once and then move on to the next big idea in your life. Your superpower isn't a passing fancy or a fad.

Your superpower shouldn't be something that hangs on your wall, next to your diploma. Part decoration. Part conversation piece. This is the difference between superpower 2.0 and superpower 3.0. Superpower 2.0 exists in your mind. Superpower 3.0 exists in your hands and your feet.

Your superpower should be front and center. It should be doing work on your behalf. Let me say that again—Your superpower should be doing work on your behalf. Every. Single. Day.

Your superpower is a tool. It's not your only tool, but it is your most powerful. Use it often. Use it with intention and full awareness. Make your superpower part of your every day. Make it part of your big decisions. Allow your superpower to influence every significant action, or inaction, in your life.

If you don't, then you don't really have a superpower. You have a parlor trick.

Getting to 4.0

◆◆◆

If you've finished the work to get your superpower upgraded to version 3.0, then you now have something that is potent and powerful. Your superpower is not only a source of pride in your life, it's doing a significant amount of work on your behalf. You might not wield your superpower every day, but you are aware of it every day. The people around you are getting a sense of your superpower and they like what they see.

This all sounds pretty good. Does that mean we're done?

Not quite.

Like any tool, superpowers require routine maintenance. They require troubleshooting from time to time. We may feel comfortable using our favorite tool, but we can always get better. The road to mastery is a long one, if not a never-ending one.

Getting to 4.0 means answering the question:

How can I optimize my superpower?

Reflect Regularly

◆◆◆

Life can only be understood backwards;
but it must be lived forwards.
- Soren Kierkegaard

Chances are, you're going to be using your superpower a
lot. Every time you do, you'll have a golden opportunity to
learn from the experience. What worked? What didn't?
What would I do differently next time?

The US military is known for their use of the After Action
Review (AAR) process. At the end of each mission, the
whole team comes together and analyzes what went well
and what didn't. The process is set up in a way as to be
totally non-threatening. The goal isn't to point fingers or
lay blame. The only goal is to learn and to improve.

You should develop a habit of performing an AAR every
time you use your superpower. Ask yourself:

- What was supposed to happen?
- What actually happened?
- What might have contributed to the difference
  between the expected results and the actual results?
- What level of superpower intensity did you bring?
  Was that too much, too little, or just enough?
- What did you learn about the limits of your
  superpower?
- What can you do to expand and enhance your
  superpower to reduce the chances of hitting these
  limitations in the future?

When it comes to after action review, the power is in the process. By using a formal evaluation process, you'll be able to step outside of your own frame of reference so that you can do an objective assessment of your superpower performance.

Best Practice #1 - Keep a journal

People cringe when I tell them to keep a journal. It feels like work. It is work. It takes more time and effort to write down your thoughts than it does to merely think about the situation.

Don't just conduct the After Action Review in your head. Doing this is better than nothing, but it's definitely cheating. The act of writing engages different parts of your brain. Writing forces you to think objectively. It carves the grooves of your experience deeper into your psyche. The more you engage, the more you learn.

Another benefit of journaling is that you will maintain a record of what actually happened. Our memories are fragile and selective. Our memories are revisionist history. You may think you have a fantastic memory. *Like a steel trap, I tell ya.* Trust me. You don't. Nobody does. Nobody except my wife, of course. (Love you honey!)

When you write something down, there's no debate. You have an objective record of exactly what you were thinking at the time. I don't go back and read my old journals very often, but when I do, I'm always amazed at the difference between my memory of the past and my words on the paper.

But even if you never go back and reread your old journals, there's value in the process. There's value in capturing your reflections in a formal, methodical way. Do it a few times and you'll see the benefits yourself. Guaranteed.

Best Practice #2 - Get a second opinion

In addition to your personal reflections, sometimes it's helpful to get the perspective of outside observers. It's not always easy to do this and it will never feel like there's enough time, but it's worth the effort, especially if the situation was something important, or if the outcome was something different than what you expected.

Asking for feedback is always a scary proposition, particularly if things didn't go well. Asking for feedback about your superpower may feel strange and awkward. Of course, you don't have to mention your "superpower." You can simply ask for feedback on how you performed throughout the situation. What did you do well? What would they suggest you change for next time?

Most people will be happy to help in any way we ask of them. It's fear that prevents us from asking. Remind yourself that feedback is not about blame, it's about growth and development. Feedback is about making yourself stronger.

Also, there is only one appropriate response when someone offers you the feedback you requested: "Thank you. I really appreciate your feedback."

Each application of your superpower is a unique opportunity to learn and to grow. Don't waste any of them.

***

Additional Resources

Check out the **After Action Review** worksheet in the Digital Appendix.

www.superpower50.com

Remember to Stretch

◆◆◆

I am always doing that which I cannot do,
in order that I may learn how to do it.
- Pablo Picasso

There was a time in my life when I played a lot of golf. I was never a great golfer, but I was better than average. There was a stretch when I was playing really, really well. My scores were the lowest they'd ever been and I was confident in my game. I couldn't wait to show off to my buddies at our annual golf trip.

Of course, it didn't work out that way. I played horribly. I blew up like The Godfather. It was as if I had gone backwards. My skills had regressed. I was completely bummed. When I tried to explain to my buddies how well I had been playing, they just smiled and nodded. I was so disappointed in myself. To make matters worse, as soon as I got back to my home course, I went right back to where I was before I left for the golf trip. I was crushing it again.

What caused my terrible performance during the golf trip? The problem wasn't the pressure. The problem was in my preparation. In the months leading up to our golf trip, I played the same course over and over again. My home course was comfortable. I knew it like the back of my hand. I knew exactly where to hit each shot to get the best bounces and the best lie for my next shot. I had the mental models of what a good shot should look like and my body was able to produce those shots on demand.

Those mental models didn't work once I set foot on a new course. A new course brought me to my performance edge. This isn't a problem for most golfers, because playing new courses is part of the game. But I had lost my edge. I had gotten myself into a hurtful cycle. I would have a good round and feel good about myself. Then I would go back to the same course, in an attempt reproduce the good feelings and I'd play even better. And the cycle would start over.

I was living in my comfort zone. My expectations were inflated. Then, when my imaginary world came into contact with reality, the disparity between my expectations and my reality was both jarring and depressing. I vowed to never fall into that trap again.

So I sold my golf clubs and gave up the game forever.

Just kidding. I changed the way that I practiced. I made sure that I played a bunch of different courses, under different conditions. I'm a creature of habit and it was tough for me to break out of my habits. But it was worth the effort.

Find Your Edges

We need to constantly challenge ourselves to find our developmental edges. Sometimes it's nice to know that we're going to be successful, but it's also good to have times when we're not so confident. Whenever we have to work hard, to really stretch into our superpower, we extend our capabilities. Our superpower grows even stronger.

How can you challenge yourself to use your superpower in new and exciting ways? Look back at your past journal entries, particularly at the times when you came up a bit short. Is there an opportunity to replicate some of those scenarios in a more controlled, safe environment? You might need to move to an entirely different context. If your challenging situation occurred at work, perhaps try to find a way to practice at home, or in a social setting.

When it comes to stretching, there's a sweet spot. You want to push yourself enough to make it a little scary, but not so terrifying that you get in your own way.

**

Additional Resources

Check out the **Superpower Stretch** worksheet in the Digital Appendix.

www.superpower50.com

Superpower*ed* Problems

◆◆◆

Afflictions are but the shadows of God's wings.
- George MacDonald, Scottish author and minister

Motivational posters were all the rage in the 1990's. A vivid image, with an inspirational word and a motivational blurb written underneath. Back then it seemed like no conference room was complete without one, though I can't imagine they inspired much motivation.

I preferred the de-motivational posters, myself. They were done in the same style, but with a distinctly dark humor. My favorite one read "Pessimism: Every dark cloud has a silver lining. But lighting kills hundreds of people each year who are trying to find it."

That one always made me laugh. And now, it offers a prophetic warning about the work that we're doing here. Up to now, we've been thinking of your superpower as limitless in terms of potential. And it is. But limitless potential doesn't mean completely limitless.

Superpower design is not all fun and games. Every superpower has a dark side. I call them shadows, but really, I should call them what they are. They're problems. Superpower*ed* problems. Unless we learn to recognize and work with our superpower shadows, they will constantly catch us off guard and plunge us into darkness.

The next few chapters will explore some of the common superpower*ed* problems.

Problem: Superpower*ed* Scope Creep

◆◆◆

Ability is what you're capable of doing.
Motivation determines what you do.
Attitude determines how well you do it.
- Lou Holtz

When you tap into your superpower, it changes everything. It amplifies your ability. It maximizes your motivation. And your superpower absolutely gives you a can-do attitude. For the most part, these are all good things. But there's one little problem.

Project managers know this problem. They have a term they like to use when projects go awry. "Scope creep" is when a project starts off with everyone having a clear understanding of the project boundaries, but over time, the project grows and grows. Eventually, the project becomes so complex and unwieldy, it's doomed to fail. Scope creep is a project manager's worst nightmare. I've seen it countless times over my consulting career.

Although scope creep is devastating to a project, the irony is that scope creep is born from good intentions. It's born from the can-do attitude. *Sure, we can do that, let's just add it to the plan. One more thing? Sure, okay.* At some point, one more thing becomes one thing too many.

A similar phenomenon happens with superpowers.

Superpower*ed* scope creep occurs when you unwittingly take on tasks, responsibilities, and commitments that extend beyond your superpower. Life moves pretty fast. One thing leads to another. What starts off as something squarely within your superpower wheelhouse quickly morphs into an extended journey way out of your comfort zone. In a bad way. You get in over your head or you find yourself committed to work that you don't want to do. Or, in the worst case scenario, both.

Superpower*ed* Scope - Meet Mark

To illustrate this concept, I want to introduce you to Mark, a senior executive in the financial services industry.

Mark's superpower is: *Making connections.*

Mark excels at finding patterns within complex financial systems. He's often able to connect the dots when nobody else can. He's a very sociable guy, which makes him remarkably good at business networking. Mark is particularly good at bringing together people with diverse, yet complimentary, needs and talents. His superpower is perfectly suited for the high-flying world of finance.

Although Mark is very successful, he finds himself getting into trouble from time to time and he noticed a pattern that he traces back to his superpower. Specifically, Mark discovered that he is prone to superpower*ed* scope creep.

To arrive at this realization, Mark used the superpower rings diagram by mapping the most important elements of his work. He mapped a variety of tasks and roles, intentionally capturing some areas where he was having success as well as some areas where he was struggling.

Through this exercise, Mark noticed some connections between his superpower and the areas where he was struggling. To quote the lyrics of the 80's band, The Fix, Mark noticed that "one thing leads to another."

Mark's superpower is: *Making connections*. But it never stops there. As soon as Mark connects the dots on a complex problem or as soon as he makes an important business connection, people always want him to stick around and help take things to the next stage. They want Mark to help solve the problems and execute the projects. Why wouldn't they? Mark is smart, competent, and a great dancer to boot.

But solving problems and executing complex projects are not Mark's superpower. These things are definitely areas of talent and strength for Mark. As such, they would probably map somewhere around ring #3. But these are *not* his superpower. This is a useful distinction for Mark, because sometimes, when he gets involved in long projects, Mark's energy wanes and his attention drifts. When he gets into the outer rings, he's no longer at his best.

With this increased awareness, Mark can better monitor his commitments to make sure his scope isn't creeping.

Managing Your Scope

The word "creep" implies a lack of awareness and a lack of control. The goal isn't to restrict yourself to operating only within your superpower ring. The goal is to be intentional about when you take on responsibilities and commitments that extend beyond that ring.

Problem: Superpower*ed* Expectations

◆◆◆

We don't see things as they are,
we see them as we are.
- Anaïs Nin

Raise your hand if you've ever taught someone to drive. If Dante Alighieri were alive today, and writing the *Divine Comedy* for the first time, I'm pretty sure there'd be a level of Hell where the suffering comes in the form of having to teach a teenager to drive. Not having children, I've never had the experience, but I remember my dad's suffering well enough to know that I don't want to.

What makes teaching someone to drive so painful? It's not as though we lack basic driving skills. In fact, most of us have been driving long enough to qualify as experts. Shouldn't that make it easier for us to teach someone else? Sadly, no.

Here's the problem. We forget what it was like to be a beginner. We've accumulated so much knowledge and skill over the years that the ability to drive is part of us. We don't even have to think about how to operate, we just do it. We've achieved embodiment.

We forget that driving a car requires someone to make lots of decisions. We forget what it was like when we had to deeply concentrate on every single decision. *Okay, gas … no, no, brake! Turn the wheel gently. But don't forget the turn signal. Check your mirrors!*

Because we can't remember what it was like, we don't think to explain things to the new person in those terms. We just assume they'll figure it out and then we become frustrated when they don't. *How did you not see that mailbox? How did you not see that post office?* We take the skill of driving for granted.

Taking Your Superpower for Granted

Why would you do that? Simple. Because it's *your* superpower. You forget that not everyone can do what you do, the way you do it. In fact, *nobody* can do what you do, the way you to it. You're unique. Remember?

So what? Who cares if I forget every once in a while? What's going to happen?

The biggest risk is that you start demanding the people around you live up to the same standards that you have for yourself. Your superpower*ed* standards. You expect other people to be able to do what you can do and become frustrated when they can't. It's totally unfair. It's like getting angry at someone for not being taller.

Superpowered Expectations - Meet Sarah

Sarah knows what it's like to have superpower*ed* expectations.

Sarah's superpower is: *I step up.*

Throughout her life, Sarah has been driven by a deep sense of loyalty and commitment to the people around her and to her highest principles. When something needs doing, and nobody wants to do it, Sarah steps up.

It's a beautiful thing to see. Her friends and family love her for it. They depend on Sarah to step up. And of course, Sarah likes stepping up, so it all works out beautifully … until it doesn't. What happens when Sarah gets tired? What happens when she feels overwhelmed by the weight of the circumstances and the burden she's carrying? What happens on the days that Sarah needs help? What if nobody else steps up?

It's easy to see how Sarah might become frustrated when the people around her don't have the same superpower*ed* ability to step up.

Superpowered Awareness

For you, your superpower is completely natural. Half the time, you may not even realize that you're using it. You don't consider the fact that other people don't have the same superpower. This is a problem. You need to disrupt this default thinking. You need to develop superpower*ed* awareness.

When you are highly aware of the nature of your superpower and highly attuned to the moments when you are using it, you'll be able to catch yourself projecting your superpower*ed* expectations onto the people around you. You can adjust your expectations accordingly.

But I really do wish the people around me had a little more of my superpower in them. That's okay. The world would be a better place if everyone had everyone else's superpower. As long as you're wishing it *for* them and not *from* them. As long as you are *wishing* and not *expecting*.

The difference is huge. When we expect something and people come up short, we become frustrated. When we wish for something on behalf of someone and they come up short, we become compassionate. With compassion, comes patience.

Superpowered Excess

◆◆◆

The road of excess leads to the palace of wisdom...
You never know what is enough
until you know what is more than enough.
- William Blake, from *Proverbs of Hell*

Too much of a good thing is too much. Although when it comes to pie, my 6-year-old niece would disagree.

Your superpower is a good thing. But if you don't pay attention, even your superpower can be too much. There are an infinite number of ways this can happen, but generally they fall into one of two categories. Your superpower will become overwhelming for the people around you or your superpower will overwhelm you.

Chances are, you are more susceptible to one of these flavors, though it's entirely possible you experience both, from time to time. To help you assess your risk, we're going to explore both types of superpowered excess.

Overwhelming Others - Meet Charles

Charles knew he was born to be an accountant. There are a lot of things about accounting that turn people off. The minutia. The rules. The complexity. The issues. Charles loved all of them. He lived for them. It was no surprise when Charles identified his superpower as: *Tenacious curiosity*. Charles had found the perfect career for someone with this superpower.

When I asked Charles if his superpower ever got him in to trouble, he laughed and said, "all the time." He went on to explain that sometimes his curiosity would cause him to dive so deep into the technical accounting issues that he would fall behind on his assignments. But told me that wasn't his biggest problem. He said, "My biggest problem is that sometimes my curiosity is too much for people."

For Charles, being curious and learning wasn't enough. He wanted to share what he learned with other people. Charles wanted to share his superpower with the world. Of course, most people don't have Charles's appetite for the details. They don't have the time. To make matters worse, Charles wasn't only curious about accounting, he was curious about people. All people. He couldn't help himself. Every phone call could turn into an expedition as his curiosity ran amok. The same superpower that served him well for the core function of his job sometimes got Charles into trouble on the periphery.

Charles is a great example of how a superpower, if left unchecked, can become overwhelming for the very same people we are trying to serve. Certain superpowers, combined with certain personality styles, are more prone to this type of excess.

What about your superpower? Are you prone to get deep into the details of things when other people don't care to? Do you see things faster than everyone else, causing people to feel pressure to keep up? How does your superpower-energy level compare to the people around you? Is your superpower likely to be "too much" for the people you are trying to serve?

Overwhelming Yourself—Meet John Coffee

Before any commercial airlines flight takes off, you'll hear the following instruction: "Put your own oxygen mask on first, then provide assistance to others around you."

Why is it important that we put on our own mask first? It's simple. If we can't breathe, we can't possibly be much help to anyone else. Duh. That's obvious. But if it's so obvious, then why do the airlines feel the need to remind us every time?

It's because we're fundamentally wired to help other people, and in a moment of crisis, our natural instinct might be to selflessly help others while neglecting our own needs. By reminding us before each flight, the airlines are hoping that we remember this point, should those yellow oxygen masks drop from the compartment overhead.

Many of us need a similar reminder when it comes to our unique superpower.

Does your superpower often lead to you take on more and more responsibility and commitment? Does your superpower cause you to expend massive amounts of energy? Does your superpower point toward an unquenchable thirst to do more and to be more?

One of my favorite movies, *The Green Mile*, depicts this concept beautifully. The hero of the story, John Coffee has the ability to heal others by drawing their pain out of their body and into his own. The other person immediately feels relief, but the process takes a toll on Coffee and he often collapses from fatigue afterwards.

It is *your* responsibility to manage your superpower energy. Nobody else will do it. Nobody else can do it. You'll want to develop structures and routines for managing your superpower exertion. Build in time for rest and recovery. There will always be another day and another opportunity to use your superpower to serve the world. Make sure you live to see that day.

***

Additional Resources

Check out the **Superpower Energy Management** worksheet in the Digital Appendix.

www.superpower50.com

Superpower*ed* Isolation

◆◆◆

The only real progress lies in learning to be wrong all alone.
- Albert Camus

If you ever want to feel lonely at the deepest level, lock yourself in a room with nothing but a record player and a vinyl copy of *Frank Sinatra Sings for Only the Lonely*.

Frank knew. There's nothing sadder than being alone. We are a social species. We need to be part of something. If you need proof, consider this: In prison, solitary confinement is the worst punishment. There's nothing worse than feeling alone.

What happens when your superpower causes you to feel alone in the world?

The Lonely Truth - Meet Will

Will knows how lonely a superpower can be.

His superpower is: *Bringing voice to the truth.*

As Will can tell you, sometimes the truth is inconvenient. Sometimes people don't want to hear the truth because they are happier with their illusions. Sometimes, the truth requires you to stand alone. There are days when Will is forced to make an agonizing decision—*Do I choose to live authentically, or do I choose to live easy?* For Will, it's rarely easy.

Most of the time, your superpower will connect you and bring you closer to the people around you. But there may be times when the uniqueness of your superpower shines a light on the gap between you and everyone else. You'll wonder why they can't do what you do. Why they can't understand what you do. Why they don't get you.

Your superpower is fundamental to your identity. Uncovering and cultivating it is a spiritual practice. It's also a lonely practice. This is the paradox of the unique soul. It simultaneously connects and isolates.

These feelings can be incredibly deep and massively impactful. Each of us is a proud island, yet we are terrified of being alone. Most of us carved this groove early on. We were taught from the earliest age that someone will always be there to comfort us. Many of us, with time, learn this is an illusion and we work to free ourselves from this dependency.

Working from an Island

What is the best way to overcome feelings of the loneliness that your superpower creates? Move toward it. Embrace it. Recognize that your isolation is a function of your uniqueness, and it's from this uniqueness that your true power emanates. Recognize that you may feel lonely, but you are never alone.

Strive to use your superpower for good and that good will be understood.

It may not be today. It may not be tomorrow.

It may not even be in your lifetime.

It may not be the people you most want to understand it, but it will be the people who most need to understand it.

Remember that solitude is not the same as isolation. Solitude isn't lonely.

Solitude is a choice. Solitude is By Design.

Embrace solitude.

Reading the Shadows

◆◆◆

Every superpower has its weakness. Just as each superpower is unique, so too is its Kryptonite. We need to be deeply attuned to the ways that our unique superpower can help us and the people around us, but we also need to be aware of how our superpower can get us into trouble.

You can't do everything.

You can't expect others to do what you do.

You can't allow solitude to become loneliness.

Too much of a good thing is still too much.

Read the room.

Put your oxygen mask on first.

You will make mistakes. Your superpower is strong, but it isn't magical. Own your mistakes and learn from them so that you don't repeat them.

Be intentional about how and when you wield your superpower.

Watch for shadows. When you find them, shine a light on them.

Broadcast Your Message

◆◆◆

Brand is just a perception,
and perception will match reality over time.
- Elon Musk, Co-Founder & CEO, SpaceX

If a tree falls in the woods and nobody's around to hear it, does it make a sound? If you have a superpower and nobody knows about it, do you really have a superpower?

Sure, it's possible that people can experience the benefits of your superpower and never realize that it is *your* superpower. That's the way Clark Kent did it. People got the benefits of Superman, but never made the link to Clark. We were okay with this. In fact, it made us love Superman even more. Who doesn't love a humble hero?

In real life, it doesn't work like this. Anonymity is not a good long-term strategy. In real life, you're better off if people know about your superpower. You're better off if everyone knows about it.

Most people cringe at the idea of "marketing" themselves to the world. It feels cheesy. It feels sleazy. It feels simultaneously arrogant and terrifying. *It's so much easier to keep this whole thing a secret. Why can't we just do that?* The reason is simple.

People need to know how you can help them in order for you to help them. They might not realize that you are in a position to help them. They might not realize there's someone walking around with a superpower like yours. Plus, most people don't go around advertising their problems with the hopes that someone with the perfect superpower will appear.

Great things happen when you let people know about your superpower. They'll appreciate the value you have to offer. They'll find ways for you to add value to their lives. They'll tell colleagues, friends, and family members, giving you the opportunity to add value to their lives too. Once people find out about your superpower, they will line up at your door to help you use it.

Do What Feels Natural

How do you tell people about your superpower in a way that feels natural and authentic?

You might worry that people will hear the word "superpower" and they'll think you're crazy. They won't. They'll be curious. They'll want to hear more about your story. As long as that story is authentic and appropriate for the audience, they will listen. They'll be thrilled to listen.

That said, you might need to tweak your language a bit to reach a particular audience. There's no rule that says you need one single description of your superpower for every situation. We want people to focus on the superpower, not the fact that you *have* a superpower. Consider these different variations on the same superpower:

Suppose your superpower is: *I unlock the potential.*

You have a knack for helping other people discover their talents.

You are at your best when you're making the people around you successful.

At this point in your life, you're really focusing on helping others to grow.

You'd rather make an assist than score a goal.

I'm sure you can imagine a dozen other variations on the same. A good superpower description does two things:

1) It instills a sense of motivation and pride in you. If it does, others will pick up on this.
2) It gives the people around you a sense of how you can be of service to them.

Once you start practicing telling people about your superpower, you'll notice there are lots of opportunities to tell your story. Job interviews. Performance review conversations with your boss. Even over a cup of coffee with a friend who might be struggling with something that's right in your wheelhouse.

The more you practice, the more you'll refine your technique. The more you practice, the more opportunities you will see. At first it may feel strange and inauthentic, but after a while, you'll find your unique way.

Make it Subtle

In advertising, there's obvious and there's subtle. Obvious is putting up a billboard or taking out a 30-second commercial spot during the Super Bowl. Subtle is skillful product placement in the background in a movie scene. Subtle doesn't mean unintentional. Subtle doesn't mean ineffective. Done well, subtle is powerful. But there's an art to subtle.

As you know, Getting to 1.0 and Getting to 2.0 are largely about language. You've put a lot of thought into choosing the right words to name your superpower. How often do you use those words in daily conversation?

I'm not suggesting you need to put up a billboard. You don't need to walk around saying: "Did you know my superpower is unlocking the potential in any situation?" That would be obvious and awkward. Subtle might look something like this: "I really think we have an opportunity to unlock some hidden potential with this project."

What would happen if you found ways to subtly start using your superpower language? Would people start to associate those words with you? You better believe it. And the more you use the words, the more they will associate those words with you. Words have a powerful associative quality.

More importantly, each and every time you use your superpower language, your ownership will get stronger and stronger. Your superpower will get stronger and stronger.

Strive for Consistency

When it comes to marketing your superpower, the most important thing is consistency. Are you consistently finding ways to use your superpower? Are you walking your talk? Are you delivering on your commitments?

People remember actions more than words, so make sure your actions are congruent with your superpower messaging.

Create a Workout Plan

◆◆◆

I am building a fire, and every day I train,
I add more fuel.
- Mia Hamm

It's easy to slip into a comfortable mindset about your superpower. Consider this tennis analogy. Your superpower is your forehand. Because it's the one part of your game that you've got down pat, so you might focus all of your attention on your weakness—your backhand.

Don't get me wrong. Working on the weak spots in your game is important. It's critical. At the same time, don't take your strengths for granted. Your superpower is the strongest part of your game. It is your differentiator. You should constantly be looking for ways to make it even stronger. Looking for ways to push your limits.

Be intentional about improving your ability to wield your superpower. This means regularly pushing the envelope and consistently reflecting on how things go each time you use your superpower, just like we talked about earlier.

It also means creating an intentional approach for developing your technique. Think of this as a workout routine for your superpower muscles. Design experiments. Read books. Find mentors who have a similar superpower. Design practices that will help work the superpower muscles that you'll need when "stuff" really goes down.

Be intentional about how you cultivate and care for your superpower. Design a program that will put you on a continuous cycle of practice, application, reflection, and recovery.

There's almost no wrong way to do this, other than to not do it at all.

Intention first. Everything else follows.

From 3.0 to 4.0

◆ ◆ ◆

To plant a garden is to believe in tomorrow.
- Audrey Hepburn

My wife and I recently did a landscaping project in our small backyard. At the center of our garden is a Japanese Lilac tree. When it blooms, the leaves turn an ivory white and the air fills with a sweet perfume. It's beautiful, but it's very small. When the landscapers transplanted the tree into the yard, I was disappointed.

"That's not going to provide much shade," I commented. The landscaper shook his head. "Not for about 8 years. But then it will be absolutely beautiful."

This set me on a path of reflection. I realized how rarely I take a long view in my life. I think I'm like most people, focused almost entirely on the near term. I tackle the problems of today and maybe tomorrow. I don't do a lot of planning for the distant future.

This is the difference between superpower version 3.0 and superpower version 4.0.

It's easy to think of your superpower as a here and now thing. But your superpower is also a tomorrow thing. And a next day thing. And the next year. And the next ten.

If you want your superpower to grow, you need to feed it. If you want your superpower to adapt to the changing environment, you need to maintain it.

Superpower design is a lifelong project.

Getting to 5.0

◆◆◆

If you're solidly operating from superpower version 4.0 then you've got a lot of really good stuff happening in your life. Not only do you have a superpower that motivates and inspires you, but you've also found ways to put it to work in the world. The people around you know what you're up to and they are fully on board.

You are acutely aware of your superpower abilities and your limitations. Of course, life won't always cooperate and sometimes you'll get yourself into trouble. But luckily, you've become an expert troubleshooter.

Each and every day you are working hard to make sure your superpower is working hard for you.

What else is there? How can there possibly be anything better than this? Well, there's one more important question that you need to answer and that's what superpower version 5.0 is all about:

What is the point of all this?

Define Your Essence

◆◆◆

The present letter is a very long one,
simply because I had no leisure to make it shorter.
- Blaise Pascal

Where does your superpower come from? This is where the comic book superheroes have it easy. The origin of their superpower is obvious. Superman was born on another planet. Wonder Woman was sculpted from clay and then brought to life by the gods. Spiderman was bitten by a radioactive spider. What I wouldn't give to be bitten by a radioactive spider. Life would be so simple.

Mere mortals, like you and me, need to search deeply if we want to discover the source of our superpower. Our superpower doesn't come from some external source, it comes from within us. To find the source, we're going to need the superpower rings diagram that we've been working with since way back when.

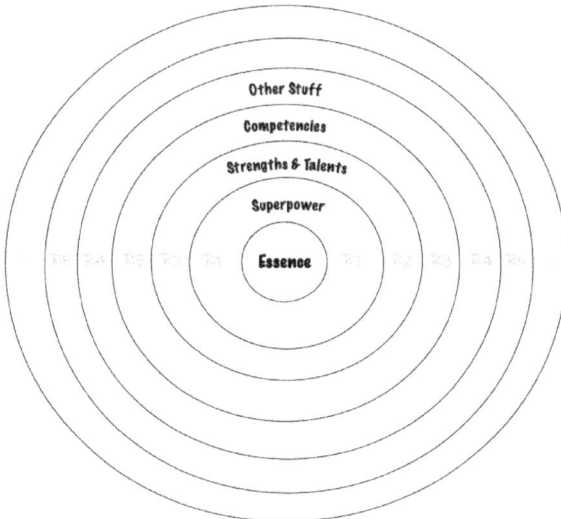

Do you notice a difference? Look at the center. Up until now, the center of the superpower rings has been you. Now there's a strange word in the center: **Essence**.

What does it mean? Here's the definition from Dictionary.com.

Essence (noun): the intrinsic nature or indispensable quality of something, especially something abstract, that determines its character.

Your essence is your indispensable quality. Your essence determines the character of you. In many ways, essence defines you. It tells you why you are here. I know, that's deep. It's hard to grasp the concept at first. It's a little easier if we think about essence in context of your superpower.

Your essence enables your superpower. Without your essence, your superpower would not exist. Essence is the fuel that drives your superpower. Your superpower is your essence in action.

Your superpower tends to be more visible and tangible. You, and people around you, can point to it when it happens. Essence, on the other hand, is always there, but in the background. That's why it's easier to start by getting a sense of your superpower first, and then look deeper to discover the essence that drives your superpower.

What Does Essence Look Like?

I need to declare something up front … I'm a bit new-age'y. I've been trying to hold back to this point, but I can't do it any longer.

Sometimes I think of essence as energy. If this were a movie, your essence would appear as a soft glow of light, surrounding you wherever you go. You'd be able to see your own essence. You could feel the essence of the people around you and they could feel yours, but it would be very subtle.

Of course, this isn't a movie. We must rely on words to describe our essence. Unfortunately, words will always come up a bit short. Even when you come up with a fantastic word to express your essence, it might feel as though something is missing. Thus, true understanding of your essence is for you, and you alone. That said, we need to work with what we've got.

Take a look at your superpower. What is one word, one attribute of you, that allows that superpower to exist? When trying to name your essence, it's usually helpful to describe it as a single word. Like an irreducible fraction.

I opened this chapter with a quote. As a writer, it's one of my favorites. Pascal is telling us that it takes more effort to communicate efficiently than it does to ramble. We use more words when we don't understand something. If you need to explain it to yourself, it's not essential. Essential doesn't require explanation.

Find one word to describe your essential core.

Some Essential Examples

I want to offer a word of caution here. I realize the concept of essence may be abstract and require an example or two. The problem is that a person's essence is so personal, much of the meaning is lost, especially if you don't know the person. That said, for illustrative purposes, it will probably work best if I use some well-known historical figures and we imagine what their superpower and essence might be.

Keep in mind, I've never met any of these people and it's impossible to determine someone else's superpower, let alone essence, by merely observing them. Superpower discovery is something that happens from within. In fact, you'll probably feel how these fabricated examples fall short of what you know about these people. That's because the examples are coming from me, not from the true heroes.

Arnold Schwarzenegger - No matter what you think of *The Terminator*, it's easy to appreciate the things that Arnold has accomplished, particularly in his early years. I can imagine his superpower might be something like: *Overcoming impossible obstacles*. What kind of essence would fuel that kind of superpower? Maybe something like: *Persistence* or *Commitment*.

Mother Theresa - I'm no expert in Mother Theresa's life, but I picture a woman choosing to work in the slums of Calcutta, helping the poorest people in the world, and I can imagine her superpower being something like: *Seeing the light through the darkness*. Wow. That feels lofty, right? What could possibly fuel a superpower like that? How about: *Hope* or *Optimism*.

George Washington - I'm not a historian, so my understanding of the first president of the United States is very much a caricature. Let's pretend that George Washington's superpower is: *To lead*. What essential quality might allow him to possess such a superpower? Perhaps his essence could be: *Vision* or *Wisdom or Courage*.

What's the point of all this?

I mentioned in the previous chapter that getting to superpower 5.0 is about answering that very question. So, where does your essence fit in? On some level, essence *is* the point. Your essence is who you are and why you are. Once you know your essence, the rest is just details.

In the next chapter, I'll show you how to use essence in your life.

—

NOTE: I first encountered the concept of "essence" in Tim Kelley's book, *True Purpose: 12 Strategies for Discovering the Difference You Are Meant to Make*. Although my application of the concept is different from Tim Kelley's, his work inspired my interpretation and I felt it appropriate to reference him here. (Kelley, 2009)

Live On Purpose

◆◆◆

The soul which has no fixed purpose in life is lost;
to be everywhere, is to be nowhere.
- Michel de Montaigne

Do you believe that someone can have a purpose in life? In my business, I ask this question a lot. In my experience, most people believe in the concept of life purpose … for some people. There are so many examples that we can point to: Mother Theresa. Gandhi. Martin Luther King Jr. For each of them, their purpose is clear.

Let me ask a different question: Do you believe that *you* have a purpose? When I ask that question, I usually get a very different response. I usually get a bit of apprehension. *I'm not sure. I'd like to think so. If I do, I don't know what it is.*

It's so much easier to see the purpose in someone else's life than to see it in your own. Why is that?

I think part of the reason can be found in the quote at the beginning of this chapter. Philosopher Michel de Montaigne chose a very interesting word to describe the concept of purpose—Fixed. In my experience, most people have a similar sense of the meaning.

Purpose feels permanent. You have one purpose and that's it. It feels hugely important. MY PURPOSE. What if I get it wrong? It's daunting. I could spend half my life pursuing the wrong thing. What if I invest a whole bunch of time and it turns out I don't have a purpose at all? I'd rather not decide. I'd rather not declare. Just to be safe. It's much easier, and safer, to leave the whole purpose-thing to people like Mother Theresa, Gandhi, and Martin Luther King Jr.

I think the problem lies in the way that most of us define "purpose." We think of purpose as something that we're meant to be doing. Something that we were created to do. Destined to do. In this sense, purpose is very specific. There's one thing that *is* our purpose and everything else is *not* our purpose.

This is flawed thinking. Who does the same thing for their entire life? Nobody. The real world isn't linear. The real world is confusing. The real world is messy.

There's a better way to think about purpose.

Purpose is Plural

What if "purpose" is plural? What if it means:

> *Any enterprise that we undertake*
> *where we regularly use our essence and our*
> *superpower for the benefit of others.*

How does this feel? More achievable? More useful? One thing is for sure, this definition of "purpose" begs a different set of questions. The "fixed" definition of purpose forces us into limiting questions. *Do I have a purpose? Am I living my purpose?* The answers to these questions are either yes, or no. The "plural" definition allows us to ask a better question: *How **on purpose** am I living?*

It's no longer a binary scale. Purpose is not about yes or no. Purpose is a sliding scale. It's a range, from zero to one hundred percent.

Your Purpose

What are the two or three major enterprises that you have in your life right now? Family life. Work life. Something in your community? In each of those enterprises, how often do you get to fully express your essence? How often do you get to use your superpower? How much of a difference do these things make to your overall impact and contribution?

In other words, how **on purpose** are you living right now?

Go Beyond Yourself

◆◆◆

Real strength has to do with helping others.
- Fred Rogers

Until now, this whole superpower design experiment has been about you. Discovering your superpower. Optimizing your superpower. Presumably you are pursuing this project not only for your benefit, but for the benefit of the people around you. Perhaps being a servant to others is your primary motivation. I hope it is. If you've gotten as far as this, version 4.0 of your superpower will position you well to do just that.

Superpower version 5.0 calls upon each of us to do even more. To go even further. What might that look like? Ask yourself this question … What would change if every one of the most important people in your life knew their superpower and you, in turn, knew theirs? A lot would change. Everything would change.

When you know someone's superpower, it helps you to better appreciate where they are coming from and how they see the world. It might help you to understand why they zig when you would zag. Why they seem concerned with the details while you are trying to fly at 10,000 feet. Or vice versa.

Suddenly you can move beyond the normal emotions that we feel when we encounter someone who operates very differently than we do. Instead of feeling annoyed or frustrated, we're able to appreciate the uniqueness of their superpower and we feel curious or compassionate.

Be curious about the people around you. Ask them about their superpower. Find ways to explain how your life has changed since you began focusing on yours. You are a shining example of what superpower can do in a person's life. Share your story and help others to discover theirs. I have the confidence that you'll be able to serve them.

As you begin to encourage others to take the first steps on their superpower journey, remember what it was like in the beginning when you were first starting your journey. Don't ask them to come to you, meet them where they are right now. Remember, you began your design process as stage 1.0. Maybe even stage 0.0. That's where they are right now, so be gentle. Be patient. Be curious.

BOOK THREE

—

THE REWARD

My Life, On Purpose

♦♦♦

Choose a job you love,
and you will never have to work a day in your life.
- Confucius

It's January. I check my phone. It's warmed up since yesterday. Negative five. Fahrenheit. None of that sissy Celsius crap. This is Indiana. This is corn-fed cold. Insulated boots. Carhart jacket. Windproof gloves. Balaclava. The wind is my nemesis. But it's not enough to keep me from making the one-mile walk to the office. It's time to work.

It's a bright, sunny morning in July. I wake up, shower, dress, grab my bicycle, and head into the office. My wife is still asleep. For me, it's time to work.

We're on vacation at the beach. I get up with the sun. As I stroll down the boardwalk, I see other early risers, like me. Joggers. Walkers. Recumbent cyclist. I'm surrounded by people, yet I'm alone. Mine is the only backpack with a computer inside, because I'm going to do my work.

Las Vegas. If you like it dark when you sleep, the hotel rooms in Vegas have the most amazing window shades. Pulling them closed is like sealing yourself in a nuclear blast shelter. I always leave the shades open, just a crack. A thin line of light slices through the darkness all the way to my laptop bag, sitting on the floor on the other side of the room. Yep. Even in Vegas, it's time to work.

At this stage of my life, rarely is there a day that I don't work, though I hesitate to call it that. Work. For most people, work is something they *have to* do. They have to work because society demands it. Their life circumstances demand it. I have to work too, but not for those reasons. Don't get me wrong; I need money just like everyone else. But the need for money isn't why I do *this* work. I do this work because the universe demands it.

When I wake up each morning, there are two things that I want most. First, coffee. Coffee is always first. Then I want to do my work. I'm grateful to have found a way to align life so that I get to use my superpower every day. Bridging body and soul. It took a while. More than forty years. And nothing has been the same since. I can't imagine going back to the way it was before.

You can create this kind of alignment in your life. This doesn't necessarily mean that your job, the way you earn your living, is 100% aligned with your superpower. There are days when I don't get to use my superpower as much as I'd like. But even on those days, I'm comforted to know, that on my best days, my superpower will be the difference-maker.

No matter what you do for a living, I can guarantee there are ways that you can bring more of your superpower to the job than you are doing right now. But your superpower goes beyond whatever you do to earn a living. Your superpower has the potential to positively impact every single aspect of your life. How do I know this when I don't know you, or your superpower?

It goes back to what we've been talking about since the start. Your superpower is uniquely you, and that is a gift to the world. You are a gift to the world. And that's enough.

Superpower Service

◆◆◆

True heroism is remarkably sober, very undramatic.
It is not the urge to surpass all others at whatever cost,
but the urge to serve others at whatever cost.
- Arthur Ashe

The work of designing one's superpower is an individual undertaking. It's a collaborative effort, no doubt. But ultimately the work, and the decision to do the work, rests within each one of us.

By now, I suspect you know the reason for doing this work doesn't stop with you. It's not about you. Not in the least. But you knew that before you even picked up this book, didn't you? Yeah, I figured.

In the comic books and the movies, the superheroes all have one thing in common. They are always working for the benefit of humanity. Superpower design is no different.

In the end, I think superpower design comes down to two questions. I think life comes down to answering these same two questions.

What are my gifts?

Who are my people?

If you've made it this far, you know the answer to the first question.

Now, go find your people.

A Superpower*ed* World

◆◆◆

The future starts today, not tomorrow.
- Pope John Paul II

Our world is far from perfect.

Each year, we lose more than 45,000 lives to suicide. There are more than 2.2 million people living in incarceration. (Wikipedia) There are nearly 450,000 children in foster care. That's just in the United States.

Sometimes it seems the state of our workplace is no better. A 2017 Gallup study showed that more than two thirds of employees are either not engaged or actively disengaged in their work. The costs are tremendous. Some estimates range from 450 - 500 billion dollars annually. (Zayed, 2020)

Imagine a world where every single person recognizes and appreciates their uniqueness, while also recognizing and honoring the uniqueness of everyone else. Imagine a world where every single person knows their gifts and works hard to find ways to share those gifts with the world, each and every day. Imagine a world where every single person is tapped into an abundant energy source along with a deep sense of motivation to make a difference.

Can we create such a world? I hope so. There's one thing that I do know for sure. If we are to create such a world, it will happen one person at a time.

You are one of those people.

How do I know? Because you picked up this book.

You've drawn the sword from the stone.

That means you are worthy.

It means you care.

It means you are ready.

Now go.

The world awaits.

PROLOGUE

—

THE FINAL FRONTIER

Superpower in Organizations

◆◆◆

The strength of the team is each individual member.
The strength of each member is the team.
- Phil Jackson

Imagine working for a boss who knows and appreciates your superpower. Imagine if everyone on your team knew your superpower and you knew theirs. What would change about how the team operates? How would it impact the degree of trust that each person has in the other? How would it affect the collective trust?

The impacts would be massive. Managers could align the work and the people for maximum efficiency and impact. Each and every person would spend more time working *on purpose*. This would impact employee engagement, which would ultimately lead to increased client satisfaction.

It would create a virtuous cycle.

It is possible.

Organizations are uniquely positioned to make it happen. There are challenges, but they are manageable.

Some organizations have a prevailing culture that downplays the importance of the individual. The culture sends the message that individuals are not special. Nobody is unique. Sometimes this is subtle, but sometimes it comes down like a hammer blow.

If the organization sends the message that people are not special, people won't be special.

If the organization sends the message that power comes from the top, people won't search for the power within.

If the organizational culture is to fall in line and keep quiet, then unique voices will never be heard.

If the people are too busy living up to their obligations to the organization, they won't have time to live up to the obligation they have to their soul.

Every organization has a choice. Culture is a choice. It cannot be dictated, but culture can be cultivated. With intention, an organization can create a culture that encourages every individual to discover and celebrate their uniqueness. Organizations can turn our differences into something that we embrace and celebrate, rather than something that we fear.

Resources need to be controlled and managed. People don't. People need to be inspired and empowered.

To be part of a great team, people must first appreciate the greatness within themselves.

If you are part of an organization, you have a choice. If you lead an organization, you have a choice. The choice to stifle the soul of the individuals and thus fail to live up to the organization's potential, or the choice to ignite each individual soul, thereby liberating the greatness of the entire organization.

What do you choose?

What's Next?

◆◆◆

I mentioned in the very beginning, that Superpower 5.0 is not just a book. It is an experience. It is also an invitation. As you now know, superpower design is a lifelong project. We are each, a life-long, work-in-progress.

I hope this book has served you well. If you enjoyed it, there's more where this came from. Consider this an open invitation.

If you've accessed your Digital Appendix, then you've already been to the Life Design Center website. This is the epicenter of my work. Here you will find all kinds of resources, such as my weekly vlog - Intentional Tuesdays. You'll also find tools, online courses, and much more. If you have not done so already, please have a look around. www.lifedesigncenter.com

If you enjoy my writing style, you might also want to check out my first book: *Never Too Late: Get Unstuck, Escape Mediocrity, and Design a Life You Love*. This is a much broader look at the concept of Life Design, whereas Superpower 5.0 is a deep-dive into a single aspect. Both serve their unique purpose.

I truly hope to cross paths with you at some point in the future. Until that day...

Prosperous Journey,
-zog

References

◆◆◆

Childrensrights.org. (2020) Foster Care. URL:
https://www.childrensrights.org/newsroom/fact-sheets/foster-care/

Kelley, Tim (2009) 12 Strategies for Discovering the Difference You Are Meant to Make. Berkley: Transcendent Solutions Press.

McCarthy, Cormac. (1993) All the pretty horses /New York : Vintage Books,

Wikipedia.org. (2020) Suicide in the United States

Wikipedia.org. (2020) Incarceration in the United States

Zayed, Leila. (2020) 5 Surprising Statistics About Disengaged Employees, from URL:
https://blog.bestcompaniesgroup.com/blog/disengaged-employees

www.ingramcontent.com/pod-product-compliance
Lightning Source LLC
Chambersburg PA
CBHW051729040426
42447CB00008B/1038